A VIEW
FROM
SECOND
BASE

A COMPLETE BASEBALL
REFERENCE MANUAL
FOR BASEBALL LOVERS
OF ALL AGES

TOM HERR
Former All-Star Second Baseman

A VIEW FROM SECOND BASE
Published by:
Double Play Press
1077 Olde Forge Crossing
Lancaster, PA 17601

Printed in the United States of America by Jostens Inc.

ISBN 0-9663875-0-3

DEDICATION

To my wife, Kim, whose unselfish love uplifted me throughout my career. It takes a special woman to endure the baseball life and Kim was the best partner that anyone could have. Also, a special thanks to my two sons, Aaron and Jordan, who didn't care how I played, they loved me anyway.

CONTENTS

INTRODUCTION

Baseball has been a large part of my life. It is a game that I began playing at a very young age and enjoyed growing up with. I had the pleasure of playing the game at the highest level, a six-year minor league experience and a twelve-plus-year major league career. My appreciation of the nuances of the game has motivated me to write this manual on the proper way to play and manage the game. My intent is to cover the total game in an attempt to help players, coaches, and fans understand the great game of baseball better.

My knowledge of the game is a result of the work of many dedicated baseball people who contributed to my career over my amateur and professional experience. I would like to thank the following people whose help throughout the years has contributed to a large part of the contents of this manual: my parents Paul and Thelma, who were always very supportive during my athletic career, and my brother, Jeff, who spent many hours playing whiffle-ball with me in the back yard and introduced me to switch-hitting. Also, a special thanks to my in-laws, Pat and Dick Garman, for their support. The following coaches and managers deserve a great deal of credit for their time and expertise: Harry Wirth, my coach at Hempfield High School and American Legion coach, Tom Getz, current coach at Hempfield, Tom Burgess, Hal Lanier, Hub Kittle, Bob Kennedy, George Kissell, Buzzy Keller, Tom Kelly and Whitey Herzog. Thank you guys, for your contributions to my growth in the game over the years.

The main reason for writing this manual is that, since my retirement from playing in 1991, I have seen a lack of general knowledge of the basic strategy and execution of the game. I hope that this instruction will benefit those who wish to know the game better as players, managers, coaches, and fans. Use this book as a guide and reference to help you to better execute and understand the fundamental aspects of the game that are so important to a successful season.

CHAPTER 1

GENERAL DEFENSE

In my opinion, more games are lost because of defensive mistakes than any other reason. Common mistakes such as improper positioning, throwing to the wrong base, missing cut-off men, and botching run-downs are examples of mental mistakes that can cost a team valuable runs that may result in a loss. Physical errors such as booting a ground ball or making an errant throw are a part of the game that will always be there. These types of mistakes can be improved upon through various drills and practice, but perfection in these areas is unattainable. The mental side of the game, however, is an area where simple corrections can result in saving runs.

An obvious place to start when setting up a defense is to examine the personnel available to play the various positions. All great defensive teams seem to have the common denominator of strength up the middle. These positions include the catcher, pitcher, shortstop, second baseman, and center fielder. Good defense starts with the pitcher. A guy who works fast, throws strikes, holds runners on well, and fields his position will find that his team plays much better behind him. A solid catcher is a must for a successful defense. This position requires a strong arm coupled with a quick release as well as the ability to block balls in the dirt. A team's catcher should be a leader on the team, someone with the mental toughness to endure the rigors of the position. The shortstop-secondbase combination is also a vital cog on a solid defensive club. These positions require much athletic ability, such as a strong, accurate throwing arm, good speed and quickness, and an alertness tuned into the situations that can arise during the game. The center fielder must be a player who can "go get it". This guy has to be able to cover both gaps and possess a strong, accurate throwing arm.

What I have found at the lower levels of baseball is that the manager finds out who his best offensive players are and then plugs them in to various defensive positions. This method is fine for those players who possess good all-around skills, but the key defensive positions should be filled with players who can execute defensively. Remember that good pitching and defense will stop good offense most of the time. Teams that consistently win are those which give the opposition the fewest outs to work with.

The remaining positions can be categorized as more offensive. That is, the positions where good offensive players with inferior defensive skills might be tried. This is not to say that these positions are not important to the defensive success of a team. The ideal situation for any team is to field a team that is strong at every position. Obviously a manager must make do with the talent available to him, with a premium placed upon the key defensive positions.

Perhaps the most important job that a coaching staff has during a game as far as the defense is concerned is the positioning of the players on the field. By this I mean, at what depth should the various players be as situations change during a game? At lower levels of the game the most common mistake is that position players more or less play in the same spot regardless of who the hitter is or what the game situation is. This error can be addressed by applying some basic common sense to the situation at hand.

Generally speaking, there are four depths that can be played on the infield. The first (#1) is back or normal depth. The second (#2) is double play depth. The third (#3) is infield in to about two steps behind the baseline. The fourth (#4) is infield in to the cut of the infield grass or about two steps in front of the baseline. These four depths will cover any situation that must be defended against. The catch is, when do you employ the various depths?

Depth #1 - This is the position that the infield should be in to start an inning or anytime there are no outs with the bases empty or with two outs and a force play at second or third. The deeper the infielders can play the better. This is predicated on arm strength and the speed of the hitter. For example, an infielder can play much deeper for a slow power hitter than he can for a speedy lead-off man. The more you know about the hitter, the easier it is to defend him. If adjustments are made for a particular hitter such as playing a clean-up hitter to pull, the infielders should move or adjust as a unit, that is, the shortstop may shade the hitter a couple steps toward the hole, so the second baseman should also move a couple steps up the middle.

Normal depth should be at or near the outfield grass at a distance that the infielder can still make a strong, accurate throw. The third baseman will have to do the most adjusting in normal depth depending on the game situation, score, type of hitter and speed of the hitter. For example, his normal position early in the count may be even with the bag to protect against the bunt. When the same hitter has two strikes on him, the depth should then change to deeper because the threat of the bunt is now remote. The first baseman may also have to adjust

11

in towards the hitter if a left-handed hitter poses the threat of a bunt. This adjustment is minimal however, because he does not have to make a long throw after fielding the bunt and therefore does not have to play in as close as the third baseman might have to. Another factor that is very important for fielders to consider is the count on the hitter. Depth on the corners should change according to the count as mentioned earlier, and positioning such as "straight away", "pull", etc. should also change. For instance, a hitter is much more likely to pull the ball when he is even or ahead in the count than when he is behind in the count. Positioning left and right should be done accordingly.

Depth #2 - This is the depth that infielders should play when the double play is in order, that is, when the opportunity to turn a double play exists. This depth is always closer to the hitter than #1 for all infielders. The reason for playing shallower in this situation is simply so that the ground ball gets to the infielder quicker, affording him a better chance to turn the double play. Middle infielders should move about ten feet closer to the hitter. From this position they should then move about six to eight feet closer to second base. This positioning gives the effect of the middle infielders "pinching" up the middle. By playing closer to the bag, the middle infielder can now get to the bag quickly to receive a throw in a more controlled fashion as opposed to having to run a great distance to catch the throw while running across the bag. It is nearly impossible for a second baseman to pivot and throw to first if he is running across the bag to catch a throw. The shortstop can get away with more movement across the bag because his momentum is carrying him towards first.

In depth #2 the corners should position themselves about two to four steps behind the baseline according to the speed of the hitter. Some situations may warrant the infielders to remain in depth #1 even when the double play is in order. An example of this might be when your team is ahead by a comfortable margin late in the game and the manager chooses to play deep and make sure of an out on any ground ball. Obviously, playing closer to the hitter in depth #2 limits the potential range of the infielders, but the up-side of turning a double-play to get out of an inning makes this risk acceptable.

Depth #3 - This depth is used to cut down a run at the plate in primarily two situations when a runner is at third base. The first situation would be when the bases are loaded and the manager feels that the chances to turn a double play are not good, so he opts to take the force out at home and save a run. For this situation the

13

depth should be as deep as the infielder's throwing arm strength permits. The other situation is more difficult to predict, but important nonetheless. With a runner on third and no outs, the defense can play back and concede the run or it can play depth #3. Usually early in the game it is wise to concede the first or even the second run of the game by keeping the infield back. This ploy was nearly always used by Whitey Herzog, one of the game's finest strategical managers. The theory is that your team has to score a run to win the game anyway, so that first run conceded to the other team is not that crucial. This strategy becomes more difficult the deeper into the game you are. Naturally each run you concede to your opponent means that you believe that your team can score one more than that to win.

Depth #3 should be considered later in the game when the potential tying or winning run is on third base with no outs, and in some cases, with one out. Remember that depth #3 is two to three steps behind the baseline. Why play this deep with the tying or winning run on third? Because any coach who knows the game will tell his baserunner on third, with no outs, to "make a ground ball go through". The reasoning for this is that it is too risky to send a runner home with no outs when you still have two more chances to drive him in. Thus, depth #3 allows the infielder to play deeper than the baseline and increase his range as opposed to playing all the way in to the grass, or #4 depth. This depth also allows the infielder to make a play at home should the runner try to score because he is close enough to the catcher to make a strong throw. In the event that the runner holds, the infielder merely checks the runner and takes the out at first. With one out and a runner of importance at third, things are not as predictable. The coach could choose to tell the runner to "go on any groundball to the infield" or he could stay with "make it go through". This will probably be determined by the speed of the baserunner on third and who the on deck batter is. More often than not, the runners will attempt to score with one out unless the batted ball is a "rocket" hit right at someone. As you can see, depth #3 will take some work to determine the proper positioning of the infielders because each one has different arm strength and ability to cover ground.

Depth #4 - This depth is used with a potential tying or winning run on third, one out, and a tag play at the plate. If there is any doubt if the runner is going to attempt to score from third with one out, than #4 should be employed to make sure that the run is cut off at the plate in the event he goes. By playing even with the infield grass, the fielder can quickly catch the ground ball and make the throw home in plenty of time for the catcher to make the tag. Depth #4 should never be used in a "make a ground ball go through "situation! Remember, the closer that you play to a hitter, the better chance you give him to find a hole.

Sometimes managers choose to take chances with their infields early in games. I mentioned earlier that Whitey usually always kept his infield back and conceded the first run. Roger Craig was one particular manager who did things a different way. Roger, an ex-pitcher, detested conceding anything to the other team, let alone a run! He chose to bring his infield in early in the game to cut that first run off at the plate. I do not agree with this strategy for a number of reasons, but I will say this; that as a hitter I was more relaxed hitting with the infield back than I was with the infield in. The reason is that I knew that just about any ground ball would score a run with the infield back. With the infield in however, I felt like I needed to hit the ball hard in the holes or hit a fly ball to get the run home. I prefer Whitey's strategy because I feel that the potential to create a big inning for the opponent is greater when you pull the infield in and thus limit the range of your infielders on ground balls. You also create more space between the infielders and the outfielders with the infield in so that line drives or flares hit to the outfield have a greater chance of dropping in. Plus, if the hitter has good speed and reaches base because of the pulled in infield, the potential for him to steal a base and get himself into scoring position has arisen. Whichever way a manager chooses to play his infield, he should do so fully recognizing the risks involved at that part of the game. A good knowledge of the opposing hitters is essential for making the correct call.

Up to this point, I have discussed only infield positioning on defense. Obviously, the outfield positioning is crucial as well. The key point for outfielders to remember almost always is to keep the double play in order. More multiple-run innings are caused by outfielders throwing to the wrong base than you would think. Take this scenario - with a fast runner on first and no outs, the batter hits a ground ball single to right. The baserunner aggressively attempts to advance to third base as the rightfielder charges the ball and comes up throwing to third. The throw sails high, missing the cutoff man (shortstop). The runner beats the throw to third while the batter/runner continues on to second base when he sees the throw miss the cutoff man. The next batter hits a ground ball to second, scoring the man from third and advancing the runner on second to third. The following batter then hits a sacrifice fly to center to plate the second run. The following hitter goes deep for the third run of the inning before the final out is recorded on a strikeout. Let's examine the mistakes that resulted in what should have been a one run inning. First of all, the outfield should have been playing at a depth deep enough to maximize coverage of the gaps to prevent an extra-base hit. Let's assume that this was the case in this situation. The right fielder should be thinking ahead of time that his chances of throwing out the fast runner on a ground ball base hit are not good. The prudent play for him to make would have been to throw the ball to second base to keep the batter/runner at first. The next hitter's ground ball to second would then produce a double play, hopefully, with the runner on third scoring. The fly ball to center would end the inning. His next mistake, once he committed to throw to third, was to overthrow the cutoff man. A low throw through the cutoff man probably would have held the batter/runner at first. This is just one simple illustration of how outfield mental mistakes can cost a team runs.

There are various theories as to how to position outfielders. The first area that I would like to discuss is depth of the outfielders. Generally, the centerfielder is the best athlete in the outfield. His speed and instincts are usually superior to the left- and rightfielders. Because of this, he can play a shade shallower than the other two. The outfielder on the "pull" side of the hitter should play the deepest and the "opposite field" outfielder should be shallower than the pull outfielder. This is especially true at the lower levels of the game due to the fact that most young hitters display only pull power while their opposite field fly balls tend to be weaker. There are really no set distances from the hitter that can be used. The manager can use such common sense indicators as the size of the hitter, where is he batting in the order, past results, etc. A common mistake that I have observed is that managers will play their outfield to pull just because a hitter may have pulled the ball the first time up. Hitters' tendencies take some time to figure out, and other variables enter into why hitters hit balls to certain areas such as pitch type, pitch location, count, etc. When you do feel like you have a "book" on the hitter, then you can more comfortably move your outfielders according to how you are going to pitch them. If a certain hitter pulls everything off-speed, but hits hard stuff the other way, then the outfielders should be tipped off as to what type of pitch the pitcher is going to throw. This can be done by the infielders giving a sign to the outfielders after the catcher has given the sign to the pitcher. One way to do this is for the infielder to put his glove behind his back on off-speed pitches. When the outfielder sees this he can adjust his position accordingly. Be careful not to tip off the opposition by moving too soon. I feel that this tip-off method should be used at all times because generally most hitters will tend to pull off-speed pitches.

Another good way for outfielders to predict where hitters are most likely to hit the ball is to watch where the catcher sets up for the pitch, especially fastballs. A hitter is more apt to pull a pitch that is inside and go the other way on a pitch outside. Once the outfielder sees where the catcher is setting up, he can "cheat" to one side or the other depending on the location. Obviously, the control of the pitcher is crucial to this method of outfield play. If an outfielder sees that his pitcher can put the ball where the catcher wants it, then he can be comfortable moving accordingly.

Many managers prefer to play their outfields deep all the time. The rationale here is to try to keep everything in front of you so as to eliminate as many extra-base hits as possible. If your team is playing this way, then keep in mind that your chances of throwing out baserunners attempting to take an extra base are slim on ground ball base hits and decreased on line drive base hits. Most major league teams employ a strategy that plays the outfield deeper when trying to protect a lead later in the game, say, the sixth inning on. Usually a sign will come from the dugout that tells the outfield to back up to a point where nothing short of a homerun will get over their heads. This "no doubles" sign can also be given at any point in the game with two out and a man on first to prevent that man from scoring on an extra-base hit. Another essential sign that comes from the bench to the defense is the "all throws to second-base " sign. This sign should be given to the shortstop and second baseman who then relay the sign to the outfield. The purpose of this ploy is to make sure that the double play stays in order. This play can be used throughout the game in situations where the manager feels that keeping the chance to turn a double play is important or when he feels that his outfielder's chances of throwing out a baserunner are slim. When protecting a lead of two or more runs late in the game, this sign should be automatic because the idea is to not allow the other team to have a big inning as discussed earlier in the chapter.

The last area of defensive play that should be touched

upon is when to play the lines. This is an area of strategy of defense that has been debated for as long as the game has been played. The purpose in guarding the lines is to try to protect a one run lead late in the game. By placing the third baseman and first baseman nearer to the foul lines, you are eliminating the possibility of a ground-ball double down the line and keeping the batter/runner at first base. Many people do not like this positioning because far more balls are hit in the holes between third and short and first and second than are hit down the lines. Also, the "book" on a particular hitter may show that he never hits the ball down the line, so why play him there. My thinking on this subject is as follows: If your team has a pitcher/catcher combination that can prevent the stolen base, then the lines should be guarded for all hitters when trying to protect a one run lead late in the game. Also, any time the "no doubles" sign is given to the outfielders, the infield corners should guard the line. If a particular hitter shows strong tendencies to pull the ball, then the opposite field corner can play off the line, while the pull side remains on the line.

CHAPTER 2

BUNT DEFENSE

I have decided to devote a separate chapter to bunt defense because of the importance of being able to execute these plays effectively. Good teams must be able to defend against bunts for a hit, sacrifice bunts, and squeeze bunts. This will be an attempt to cover all of these facets of defending the bunting game including pitching strategies, positioning of fielders, and certain defensive plays designed to thwart the bunter.

When defending the attempted base hit bunt, there are some important things to remember. First of all, the element of surprise is on the side of the hitter. This fact makes defending a base hit bunt more difficult because the infielders cannot easily predict when a hitter may attempt a bunt. What an infielder can do, however, is anticipate the possibility of a bunt and therefore, keep himself better prepared in the event that the hitter does attempt to bunt. This anticipation is aided by having an understanding of when it is a good time to try to bunt for a hit, and a knowledge of which opposing hitters are good bunters. Most people assume that the best time to attempt a bunt for a hit is when leading off an inning.

23

I do not agree with this thinking for the simple reason that this is the time when most defenses are alert for the bunt, thus making executing one more difficult. Great bunters, such as Kenny Lofton, can get away with this because of their proficiency coupled with their speed. Most successful bunts occur at times when the defense is least expecting it.

The easiest way to protect against a bunt is to play the third baseman close to the hitter. When an exceptional bunter is at the plate, the third baseman should be anywhere from five to ten feet in front of the baseline and shaded toward the line. The reason for shading the line is that he has help from the pitcher on his left. This positioning obviously limits the third baseman's range on a ground ball, but often times is a necessary evil. Exceptions to this positioning are when the hitter has two strikes on him or when the tying or go-ahead run is on second base with two outs. It would not be a good time to bunt in this situation so the third baseman can play back at normal depth. The best advice that I could give to a third baseman would be to watch the hitter closely as he prepares himself in the batter's box, as sometimes hitters will tip off their desire to bunt by looking down towards third or by moving up in the box. Also watch his bat as he strides; if his hands begin to drop into a bunting position, then charge the plate. If possible, field the bunt with the glove hand like a normal ground ball. If you must field the bunt bare handed, then take the extra step to throw the ball off of your right foot.

The pitcher can help his corner men out immensely by being quick to get off the mound to field any bunts within his range. On a drag bunt down the first base line, the following rules apply. The pitcher should break to first in an attempt to field any bunt from the batter's box to about three-fourths of the way to first. If he cannot reach the bunt, then continue to the bag and anticipate the throw from the first baseman. The first baseman must read the speed of the bunt to determine if the pitcher can get to the ball. If he sees that the pitcher can field the ball, then he can go to the bag for the throw. Any hard drag bunt to the first baseman's right should be left for the secondbaseman to charge while the first baseman covers first. This play is difficult, but not as difficult as the first baseman ranging far to his right and trying to throw to the pitcher on the run to first base.

To help the defense anticipate the bunt, keep in mind when good times to bunt for a hit are. Most hitters prefer to bunt earlier in the count, or when they are ahead in the count, say 1 and 0 or 2 and 0. The reason for this is that they are more likely to see a fastball in these counts which helps their timing when bunting. Most hitters practice bunting fastballs so their timing is predicated on the pitch coming at them harder. Another good time for a hitter to attempt a bunt is with his team trailing by a run or two and a man on first. A bunt in this situation avoids a double play while possibly creating the chance for a bigger inning if successful. It is a good practice to observe the other team during batting practice to see which of the opposing players work on their bunting and which ones are proficient at it. Other good times to bunt for a hit include a man on second with no outs. A successful bunt hit here gives the offense a first and third situation with no outs and the potential for a big inning.

Defending the sacrifice bunt is more predictable and therefore should be easier to execute. It is amazing, however, how many sacrifice bunts are botched even at the highest levels of the game. One essential rule of thumb always applies to the defense in a sacrifice situation, that is " get an out". The sacrifice bunt, by definition, is the hitter sacrificing himself to advance the runner or runners. If the opposition is giving you an out, you better get it! There are four basic plays that can be employed when defending the sacrifice bunt. Which play you decide to use is dictated by the game situation, score of the game, and at what part of the game you are in. For example, early in the game a manager may choose to defend a sacrifice bunt situation differently than he would the same situation later in the game.

Normally the manager gives a sign to the catcher or one of the infielders as to which particular bunt play is on, and then that player relays the sign to the rest of the team. This can be done by designating certain areas of the body as #1, #2, etc. He gives the signs by touching various spots, with the "live" touch being the first or last sign given. The four common bunt plays are as follows:

#1. This is the most used bunt defense play. The defense is trying to field the bunt and get the out at first (#1= first base). This play is usually used with a runner on first, but can also be used with runners on first and second. If the defense suspects that the opposition may attempt a sacrifice, the corners should be in to about two to three steps in front of the baseline for play #1. With a runner on first, the responsibilities of the infielders are: **third baseman**- third baseline to pitcher's mound, then retreat back to third after the play is made;

pitcher- pitcher's mound to first baseline; **first baseman**- any ball bunted hard down the first baseline that the pitcher cannot routinely field. On bunts that the pitcher can easily get to, the first baseman should stay at first or get back to first to take the throw; **second baseman**- cover first in case the first baseman must go get the bunt; **shortstop**- cover second. The catcher must be ready to field any bunt close to home plate as well as communicating with the other fielders where to go with the throw. In the event of a terrible bunt, second base is an option, but nearly all throws should go to first on this play. This play is designed to routinely take the out that the opposition is giving up. Play #1 should be called in most bunt situations because it is the easiest of the plays to execute.

#2. This play is designed to throw out the runner going to second (#2= second base). It can be used with a runner on first or with runners on first and second. I feel that this play should be tried only when there are no outs in a sure bunt situation. A sure bunt situation is with the game tied or the opposition behind by a run in the latter part of the game. This same situation early in the game is not a sure bunt situation because some managers may opt to let their hitter swing away in an attempt to have a big inning. The purpose behind using this play is to cut down the tying or lead run at second base. On this play, the third baseman, pitcher, and first baseman all charge straight in toward the hitter. First and third go just as the pitcher is releasing the ball to home. The shortstop covers second and the second baseman covers first. The catcher can also be a factor in this play on any bunt close to home plate, as his throw to second should be an easier one to make since his momentum is carrying him towards second. If another fielder makes the play, the catcher plays "traffic cop" , telling the fielder where to throw the ball. The first look once a fielder makes the play on the bunt is to second base. If an out is available there, take it. If there is any question as to whether or not you can get the out at second, then take the out at first. Remember, "get an out". If #2 play is called with runners on first and second, the shortstop should move over toward second base early to "jockey" the baserunner back to second so that he cannot get a jump to steal third base when he sees the third baseman charge.

#3. This play is designed to get an out at third if possible (#3 = third base). This is the most dangerous of all bunt plays because a decision must be made by the third baseman whether to stay home or go get the bunt. This play can be called with runners on first and second, or second only, and is usually used early in the game when you are not as sure that the other team is going to bunt. Again, this play should be tried only when there are no outs to prevent the tying or go ahead run to reach third with less than two outs. Another rule of thumb for this play is that the pitcher should be a guy who can get off the mound quickly and field his position well. The third baseman's starting depth on this play should be way in, about fifteen to twenty feet toward home plate, in front of the baseline. From this "in" position, he must be able to get back to cover third in the event of a stolen base attempt or in the event that there is a throw to third on the bunt play. The third baseman must hold his position as the pitch is made and "read" the bunt. This is a difficult task for some third baseman because of the quick decision that must be made. If the bunt comes off the bat soft, then the third baseman must retreat to the bag for a possible play there. If the bunt comes hard down the line, the third baseman must go get the bunt and take the out at first.

The pitcher's job on this play is to cover from the mound to the third base line. The first baseman should be very aggressive on this play, starting about fifteen feet in towards home plate and off the line. As the pitch is made he should be charging hard. The second baseman covers first on play #3, while the shortstop should "cheat" over towards second base to keep the runner close. The catcher can also be very aggressive on this play and should pounce on any bunt within his range, thinking third base if he gets to the ball quickly. It is also the catcher's job to call out what base to throw to should one of the other fielders make the play.

#4. This is the "wheel" play or rotation play designed to cut down the tying or lead run at third (#4 = third base). This play should be the choice late in the game in a "sure" bunt situation. Again, remember that this play should be tried with no outs only. The rotation for the infielders is as follows: Third, pitcher, and first all charge hard. The shortstop covers third base from a starting point that positions him closer to third than normal (usually about one-half to one-third of the way to third). The second baseman holds the runner on second and then breaks to cover first. As he breaks for first, the pitcher delivers the ball home. Whichever fielder makes the play, the first option is to get the out at third, and the second option is to take the out at first.

In St. Louis, under Whitey Herzog, we ran a variation of this play that made the following changes. The shortstop "cheated" up to the base line and about 3/4 of the way to third. The second baseman held the runner on second and stayed there. The first baseman played way in towards the hitter, giving the impression that he would be charging hard. As the pitch was made, the first baseman retreated to first to cover the bag. The third baseman charged home and the pitcher covered from the mound to the first base line. The reason for this strategy was to protect against the "slug bunt", that is, the hitter faking a bunt and swinging away. In the normal wheel play the entire infield is left open, whereas in this variation the shortstop can hold his "in" position longer and cover the left side of the infield in the event of a slug bunt and the second baseman can cover the middle portions of the infield. This is a good tactic against a team that has seen you employ the wheel play or against a hitter who handles the bat very well. In both plays the catcher again should be the quarterback, yelling out where to make the throw.

At this time I would like to discuss some pitching strategies that can help to thwart the sacrifice bunt. There will be times during every game when you are not sure if the other team is going to bunt or not. Some hitters give the bunt away by squaring around early. Others disguise the attempt better by not squaring around until the pitch is on its way. One way to get the hitter to commit himself is for the pitcher to throw a pick off throw to first (with a runner on first only). When the pitcher makes his first move, some hitters begin to square around thinking that the pitcher is coming home. If they do this, you have eliminated the guesswork and now know that the bunt is on. The manager should have a pickoff sign to give to the catcher so that this strategy can be tried.

Proper bunting technique dictates that the bat be slanted upward so that the barrel of the bat is above the hands. This angle of the bat results in the ball being bunted on the ground, the desired result. With this in mind, the hardest pitches to bunt for most hitters are low fastballs or change-ups. The reason for this is that it is very difficult for the hitter to maintain the proper bat angle on a low pitch. His first instinct is to drop the barrel of the bat down to the ball, thus creating an angle where the barrel of the bat in now slanted down or below the hands. This results in a popped-up bunt. When a bunter's objective is to bunt the ball down the third base line (with a man on second), low and away fastballs are the most difficult pitches to bunt that way. Conversely, high strikes are the easiest pitches to bunt successfully because the bat angle is easy to maintain. Change-ups are hard to bunt because they throw off the timing of the bunter and often cause him to reach out for the ball.

The squeeze bunt is a very difficult play to defend,

but there are some measures that can be taken to make executing the squeeze tougher. The first tactic, if a manager suspects that the squeeze may be on, is to have the pitcher throw from the stretch and pitch out. If the squeeze was on, you have the out at home on the runner from third. If the squeeze wasn't on, at least you have planted the seed in the opposing manager's mind that you are looking for it and this may dissuade him from trying it. Another tactic is to try a pick off at third in an attempt to catch the runner leaving too early. (This tactic can only be used with a right-handed pitcher.) From his stretch position, the pitcher lifts his front leg as if he is making his delivery home. As he lifts his leg, the third baseman breaks to third for the pickoff throw. The pitcher must be careful not to break the plane of the rubber, which would force him to throw the ball home. If he breaks the plane and throws to third, this is a balk. Another tactic to use occurs when the hitter or runner gives away the squeeze too early. If the pitcher sees the hitter square around too soon, or if he sees the runner on third break for home too soon, he should automatically throw up and inside to the hitter causing him to bail out of the way. The third baseman and first baseman should charge hard when they see the runner break for home and if the bunt is hard and right at them, they may have a chance for the out at home.

The last items that I would like to touch on concerning the sacrifice bunt are special circumstances that may arise during a bunt play. Some teams, with a man on first, will start the runner during the sacrifice attempt in an effort to get the runner all the way to third. This "run and bunt" play is designed to bunt the ball to the third baseman to get him off the bag so that third base is vacated. To properly defend this play, the pitcher must be alert enough to recognize that he must hustle over to cover third when he sees the third baseman fielding the bunt. Another scenario that may arise is a popped-up sacrifice bunt. Most players merely come to the ball and make the catch for the easy, sure out. There is nothing wrong with this, but there is another alternative to consider. Often times when a hitter pops up a sacrifice attempt, he stands in the batter's box in disgust and watches the play, thinking that he is an easy out so why run. If the defense sees this, they should let the bunt drop and then pick up the bunt and make the throw to get the lead runner, and then turn the double play on the batter/runner. This is possible because the baserunner holds up when he sees the bunt popped up and the batter, as I said earlier, is not running hard to first. This is a very "heads up" play for the defense, and one that should be reviewed in practice.

CHAPTER 3

DEFENDING THE RUNNING GAME

During the years that I played for the St. Louis Cardinals we had a catch phrase that went like this, "speed kills". Speed, both offensively and defensively, is something that you cannot teach. Teams with good speed can create havoc on the base paths, using the running game as a potent offensive weapon to manufacture runs. To defend against the running game, a defensive team must execute various aspects of fundamental play in an effort to slow down the opposition. These fundamentals include holding runners close, pickoff plays, rundowns, cutoffs and relays, and pitching strategies. I will attempt to analyze these various areas in order to give the defense an idea how to control the running game.

The running game is much more than stealing bases. Good offensive teams are always looking for opportunities to take the extra base on base hits or errors, as well as stealing bases. The first area of discussion in this segment deals with cutoffs and relay throws from the outfielders. One of the most basic plays that all outfielders must make is to hit the cutoff man.

This sounds simple enough, but how often do you see throws from the outfield missing the cutoff man? This is an area of the game that should be practiced more in my opinion. One effective way to work out outfielders is to have them throwing "long toss" every day to stretch out their arms. The outfielder's goal on these long throws should always be to throw the ball to the glove side of his partner, the cutoff man. Proper positioning of the cut off men is also crucial to these plays. The following situations will cover the positioning of cutoff men during the game.

Bases empty - On any single to the outfield, the throw should be made to second base. There are two ways that the middle infielders can position themselves for this incoming throw. The first option is for one of the middle infielders to go out towards the outfielder (second baseman on a hit to right, shortstop on a hit to center and left) to receive a short throw from the outfielder, with the other infielder covering second base. This is the most commonly used method and probably the easiest way to get the ball back into the infield. One problem that I have with this method, though, is that it encourages a soft throw from the outfielder to the cutoff man. An extremely aggressive baserunner may attempt to continue on to second base, forcing two throws to get him. Another problem with this method is that if the cutoff man is missed with this softer throw from the outfield, the backup man (the man covering second) may have to leave the base to retrieve the throw, thus encouraging the runner to take the extra base. The other method used has the throw from the outfield coming directly in to second base. The second baseman covers second on a hit to right and the shortstop covers on hits to center or left. The middle infielder not covering the bag should get into a backup position about fifteen to twenty feet behind the man covering the bag. This method encourages a hard throw from the outfielder that will make the runner hold up at first. An overthrow of the bag is covered by the backup man with the bag still being covered. Difficulties can arise when trying this method when there is a ground ball hit to the outfield that the middle infielders attempt to field. It may be hard for them to get back to the bag in time to cover the throw in from the outfield. Both methods can be employed; the first used on ground ball hits and the second used on line drive hits.

On a sure extra basehit with the bases empty, the rotations used by the infielders are as follows. On a ball hit down the right field line, the second baseman goes out to be the cutoff man and the first baseman is the trailer or backup man. (These two players may switch who goes out and who backs up depending on which one possesses the stronger throwing arm.) Over throws or under throws should be left for the trailer to handle. The shortstop is the cutoff man for a potential play at third, positioning himself on a straight line from the cutoff man to third base, somewhere in the middle of the infield. The third baseman covers third and calls "cut" for the shortstop to cut and hold the ball or "relay" for the shortstop to cut off the throw and make a throw to third. If the third baseman does not make any call, the throw should not be cut off. The pitcher should be backing up third and the center fielder should be coming in to cover second base. The leftfielder should be moving over to back up third base also. The catcher stays home. When playing on a field with no fences, these extra-base hits can be potential homeruns, so the cutoff men may have to align themselves to home plate rather than third base. In the case of a ball down the right field line, the shortstop can merely adjust his cutoff position over to line up the throw to home. On all cutoff plays, if the cutoff man sees that the throw is off line, he should go cut the ball.

On "gappers", extra base hits to left center and right center, with the bases empty, the cutoff positions are as follows; (Note that these are balls that go through the gap to the outfield fence that are sure doubles at least.) On balls hit to the right centerfield gap, the second baseman goes out to be the cutoff man to a distance from the outfielder where the outfielder can make a strong, chest high throw. Obviously, this distance varies depending upon the different arm strengths of the outfielders. The shortstop is the trailer or backup man. The first baseman should follow the batter/runner to second base in case he rounds the bag too far and decides to go back. The third baseman covers third with the pitcher backing him up. On fields with no fence, the first baseman lines up to home plate. On a gapper to left center, the shortstop is first out and the second baseman is the trailer. On a sure double down the left field line, the shortstop moves over to the line for the cutoff, but not too far out, encouraging a longer throw towards third. The third baseman covers third, but is also the backup man. The second baseman covers second, the pitcher backs up third.

Man on first - Unless the manager has the "throw to second base sign" on, all singles to the outfield should be thrown to third base if there is a chance to nail the runner at third. The shortstop is the cutoff man from all fields and should line himself up accordingly. The second baseman covers second in all cases. The pitcher backs up third. Outfielders should realize that on balls that they have to range far to their left or right to cut off in the gaps, their chances of throwing out the runner advancing to third are slim. These throws should automatically go to second base to keep the double play in order with less than two outs or to keep the batter/runner on first with two outs.

On a sure double, the first objective of the defense is to prevent the runner on first from scoring. A double down the right field line has the second baseman going out for the cutoff with the first baseman trailing. The shortstop positions himself in line with home plate for the cutoff there. Another way to execute this play is for the shortstop to be the trailer and the first baseman being the cutoff man to home. I prefer the first way because the shortstop does not have as far to go to become the cutoff to home. The third baseman covers third, the pitcher backs up home, the center fielder comes in to cover second and the left fielder backs up third. As you can see there are no spectators on this play. The catcher makes the "cut" or "relay" call. If the catcher sees that the runner will score, a "cut 3" call may get the batter/runner going to third.

Gappers to right center and left center have the

second baseman or shortstop going out for the cutoff/ trailer positions. The first baseman lines up to home plate. The pitcher should "float" between third and home and read where the throw will be made and back up whichever base the throw goes to. Trailers should always be watching the baserunners behind them as they get to their backup spot so that they can communicate to the cutoff man where the next throw should go.

On a double down the left field line, the shortstop lines up to third base and the first baseman lines up to home. Some teams have the second baseman trail the shortstop so that the third baseman does not have to vacate third in the event of an errant throw from the left fielder. The pitcher backs up home and the center fielder comes in to cover second. The right fielder can back up a potential throw to second.

These relay positions hold true any time there is an extra basehit with a man on first. The situation may have other baserunners on as well, and obviously, the extra basehit will score those runners. The relays are designed to keep the man on first from scoring also.

Runner on second - The rule on basehits to the outfield with a man on second is this - with a man on second and first base unoccupied or empty, the third baseman is the cutoff man to home. The shortstop covers third, the second baseman covers second and the first baseman stays at first. The pitcher backs up home. With a man on second and first base occupied, the first baseman is the cutoff man. This is done so that the third baseman can cover third in case the throw from the outfield comes to third in a situation where the runner on first may be the more important run to deny (tying or winning run). The shortstop lines up to third and the second baseman covers second. The only exception to the "first base unoccupied" rule would be if there are runners on second and third and the batter hits a fly ball to the outfield. In this case, the first baseman would be the cutoff to home and the third baseman would stay at third in case the runner on second tags to go to third. During the course of the game, it is very important for the corner men to communicate the situations with each other so that each one knows who is supposed to be the cutoff man.

Defending against the stolen base - The most important factor in shutting down another team's stealing game is the pitcher's ability to hold runners close. This can be done in a variety of ways including varying his set time, slide stepping on his delivery, pick off attempts and stepping off the rubber. The pitcher must give his catcher a chance to throw out the base stealer. The recent trend has been for pitchers to quicken their delivery time to home plate by developing a "slide step". This is merely a delivery without the conventional high leg kick, which takes more time. This type of delivery can keep the average baserunner from attempting a steal and gives you a much better chance of nabbing the good basestealers. Pitchers should also attempt to alter their set time every pitch, as basestealers try to time the pitcher to get a better jump. Holding the ball in the set position often times causes the baserunner to tense up and diminishes his ability to get an explosive, quick jump. The pitch out is also a good weapon to show the opposition to make them aware that you are conscious of their intentions. The catcher should ready himself in a potential base-stealing situation by positioning his left foot slightly ahead of his right foot so that he can quickly step towards the target bag with his left foot and throw. The right foot remains stationary and acts as the pivot or plant foot. Catchers also need to work on a "short arm" throwing motion, that is, taking the ball directly from the mitt to the ear to throw. Pitch selection is crucial when trying to shut down the base stealer. Obviously, off-speed pitches are the easiest to steal on. High and away fastballs are a good call early in the count in running situations.

Middle infielders need to shorten up towards the hitter in potential base-stealing situations. A position about three feet closer than the normal depth with two outs and double play depth with less than two outs is correct. The shortstop normally gives the sign to the second baseman dictating who will cover on the steal. This is determined by which side the batter hits from, his tendencies, and the pitch selection. The usual method of the shortstop giving this sign to the second baseman is to cover his mouth with his glove hand so that the opposition cannot see his mouth. An open mouth sign indicates that the second baseman is covering, while a closed mouth means that the shortstop has the bag. When the second baseman is covering the bag, he should take three steps toward the hitter as he sees the runner break for second. His first step should be with his left foot, (left-right-left), so that as the pitch crosses home plate he is landing on his left foot, still facing the hitter. This enables him to plant the left foot and go to second base to cover the bag from a much closer position, thus not having as far to run to reach the bag. This technique also guards against the "hit and run" play because he is in a fielding position as the ball goes by the hitter. The most common mistake that middle infielders make when covering the steal is to run directly to second base as the runner breaks, leaving a huge opening on that side of the infield that a ground ball could get through. When the shortstop is covering, his steps are just the opposite (right-left- right). The middle infielder not covering the bag should back up the throw. On a steal of third, the third baseman's steps are identical to the second baseman's (left- right-left).

Defending the double steal - With runners on first and second, the defense must determine which baserunner is the most important or which one do you have the best chance to throw out. Often times the trail runner is the easiest to throw out because his jump is not as good as the runner on second. He must go after he sees the runner on second break for third, so he usually is a step or two behind. Also, his lead is often not as big as the runner on second.

That brings me to an area of the game where I see a tremendous amount of mistakes made, especially at the lower levels of the game; that is, holding runners on. A common mistake is infielders standing right at the bag to hold a runner close. The only infielder who should stand at the bag to hold a runner is the first baseman. A second baseman, shortstop, or third baseman standing at the bag leaves a huge hole at his particular area of the infield that enables routine ground balls to get through to the outfield. The proper technique is to "jockey" the man back by shortening up momentarily as if to go to the bag and then get back to the desired depth. As I mentioned earlier, the pitcher has the main job of keeping the runner close, not the infielders. If the pitcher feels that the runner is getting too far off, he can step off the rubber. Another mistake that I see repeatedly is the first baseman holding a runner on first with runners on first and second or even with the bases loaded! This is terrible baseball! Where can this runner go? Again, by making this mistake, the defense has created another hole for the hitter to capitalize on.

A double steal attempt with runners on first and third is a play that must be defended at all levels. There are four defensive plays that can be called for this situation. Play #1 has the catcher throwing through to second base. Times when this play should be used are when there is a slow runner on third, when you are ahead by two or more runs, when there are two outs, or anytime early in the game. The object of this play is to prevent another run from getting into scoring position by throwing him out at second. At the major league level, teams seldom try to send the man on third home because of the high risk involved with challenging strong throwing arms. At lower levels of baseball, however, this play is usually tried with the purpose of scoring the run from third. The middle infielders can execute this play one of two ways. First, they can cover the bag in the normal straddling fashion to receive the throw from the catcher. The backup man is responsible for watching the runner at third. If the runner breaks for home, the backup man yells "there he goes" and the covering infielder then leaves the bag towards the catcher to go get the throw. (The third baseman should also be yelling "there he goes".) This shortens the throw from the catcher and should enable the infielder to catch the ball and quickly return it to home. There are times when the defense may concede the run and try to tag out the runner stealing second. These would include when there are two outs or when you are ahead by two or more runs. The other method of executing #1 is for the covering infielder to go to second base and the other middle infielder getting into a cutoff position about fifteen feet in front of second base in line with the catcher. Now the cutoff man (the infielder in front) must cut the ball if he hears "there he goes" or if he sees the runner on third break for home. I feel that this play is very difficult to execute because of the split-second decision that must be made. If the runner on third does not break for home, the cutoff man lets the throw go through to second. The man covering second must always be ready to catch the ball. The catcher must always remember to glance at the man at third to make sure that the runner is not already breaking for home, in which case the catcher would merely hold the ball and make the play on the runner at third.

Play #2 has the throw from the catcher going back to the pitcher. This throw should be disguised by the catcher to look like a throw to second and thus should be thrown head high. The catcher should not look the man on third back on this play, as it is designed to trick him into leaving third base. This play concedes second base to the runner on first and is designed to catch the runner straying too far off third. This play can be used when the tying or winning run is at third.

Play #3 has the catcher throwing the ball directly to third base to attempt to catch the runner off third. Again, this option should be used when the run on third is meaningful. Another time that #2 or #3 can be used is when there is a dangerous hitter at the plate. By conceding second base, you now have an open base at first which gives you the option of intentionally walking the dangerous hitter to get to a weaker hitter.

Play #4 has the throw from the catcher going directly to the second baseman or shortstop (second baseman for a right-handed hitter, shortstop for a left-handed hitter). Whichever infielder is receiving the throw should charge directly towards the catcher from his normal or double-play depth to catch the throw moving in and then return the ball to home to get the runner breaking for home. The intent of this play is to fool the runner on third into thinking that the throw is going to second base, when in fact it is going to a charging infielder. The time to try this play is when there is an aggressive runner at third who will probably attempt to score. The catcher should again look the man back at third on this play.

A fifth option exists during the first and third steal attempt. That would be for the catcher to fake a throw to second and hold the ball. A good fake may fool the runner on third, causing him to break for home. This option can be used in lieu of numbers 2, 3, or 4, when the manager does not want to risk throwing the ball. For all of these plays, the manager relays the particular play number to the catcher, who in turn relays the sign to the infielders. Different body parts represent numbers in this system. For example, the top of the head may be #1, the face #2, the chest #3, and the leg #4. The catcher would go through a series of touches with the "live" sign being the first, second, or last touch, whatever is predetermined.

A variation of the first and third double steal is a play that has the man on first leaving early. This play is designed to score the run from third, so the defense should be aware that the man on third will always try to go home at some point during this play. This play also causes some pitchers to balk by making them flinch or jump off the mound without first stepping off the rubber. To defend the early steal properly, the defense must be alert to the play before it happens. This can be done by communicating with each other to "be alive" or "heads up" for the early steal. The first baseman should yell "step off" to the pitcher as soon as he sees the runner leave early. The pitcher steps back off the rubber and immediately checks the runner at third. In some cases that runner will have already broken for home and should be an easy out there. Once the pitcher checks the runner at third, he then turns back to the runner at first. If the runner is running hard to second base, the throw should go to the shortstop covering second base. This is probably the moment that the runner on third will break for home, so the shortstop will have to make a quick throw to home. In other instances, the base runner at first may stop halfway between first and second to try to get into a rundown. When this happens, the pitcher should throw the ball to the second baseman who should come straight in to the baseline towards the pitcher. The second baseman can then run the base runner back to first, being alert for the runner on third breaking for home. As I mentioned before, the man on third is usually instructed to break for home as soon as the pitcher makes a play on the runner at first. With this in mind, a good tactic for the defense is to have the pitcher check the runner on third and then turn to the runner at first and fake a throw, then wheel and get the man attempting to score. The worst play that the pitcher can make is to throw the ball to the first baseman when the man leaves early. The reason is that an ensuing rundown would have the first baseman running towards second and away from home plate, thus making it difficult for him to stop and make a good throw home.

In any rundown situation, three basic rules apply. First, always try to run the man back to where he came from. If he makes it back, you are no worse off. Second, the infielder with the ball should sprint after the baserunner to cause him to run hard in a particular direction. This makes it difficult for the baserunner to stop and reverse his direction. Third, hold the ball up and steady so that the infielder receiving the throw can see it. Never pump the ball back and forth, faking throws, as this will also deceive your teammate. Once you have the baserunner running hard towards a teammate, make the throw when the baserunner gets within approximately ten feet of the receiving defensive man. This will enable the man catching the ball to make the catch and tag before the baserunner can turn around. Obviously, if the man running the baserunner back can catch him without making a throw, this is better than having to throw the ball.

Another first and third play that may arise is the delayed steal. This is when the runner on first hesitates before he breaks for second. This is done to try to lure the catcher into making a panic throw to second, forgetting about the runner on third. Whichever first and third play is on at the time can still be run when the delayed steal is attempted. The catcher should look the runner back to third and make the designated throw. Some teams will have the runner on first break for second as the catcher throws the ball back to the pitcher. In this case, the pitcher should react similar to his responsibilities on the early steal play. First, check the runner on third, and then make the appropriate throw to the infielder. The delayed steal can also be used with a man on first only. Usually baserunners who are not ordinarily considered a threat to steal are the types of players who will attempt a delayed steal. The way to guard against the delayed steal is to have the middle infielders always move toward second base after the pitch passes the hitter. By doing this they are positioned close to the bag in the event that the runner on first breaks for second. Middle infielders should never drop their heads after the pitch, as this makes them vulnerable to the delayed steal.

The final situation that I would like to discuss is the "lefty play". This is a first and third situation, with a left-handed pitcher on the mound, where the offense tries to steal a run. The play is executed by having the man on third break for home just as the pitcher is coming to his set position. When the runner on first sees the man on third break for home, he tries to distract the pitcher by taking off for second or by falling down. If the pitcher makes a move to get the runner on first, the man running from third will score easily. In this situation, a left-handed pitcher should always be checking the runner on third as he is coming down into his set position. This should prevent the runner on third from breaking too soon. If he does so anyway, the pitcher can merely step off and throw him out at home.

Various pickoff plays are important for the defense to show the opposition. While pickoffs are ideally designed to throw the baserunner out, they are just as useful in keeping the offensive team from taking big, aggressive leads. If your opposition knows that you are not afraid to try pickoff plays, they will be more defensive on the bases. Conversely, too many pickoffs attempts are unnecessary and dangerous as you are risking errors anytime you throw the ball.

The basic pickoffs to first are fairly simple. A pitcher should have a feel for how much of a lead he can allow the baserunner to have. The rules state that a pitcher must step to the bag that he is throwing to on a pickoff. This step must occur before he turns his upper body. Many right-handers try to spin their upper bodies quickly, before stepping to first. This should be a balk, however some pitchers do get away with this type of move. Thus, it is important to develop a move that is quick but legal. Another option for the pitcher is to merely step off the rubber to cause the runner to retreat to first. Left-handers have an advantage with a man on first because they are facing the runner. Lefties must be careful not to break the plane of the rubber when attempting a pickoff throw to first. If a left-hander's foot goes behind the rubber during his leg kick, then he must deliver the pitch home. A balk occurs when his foot goes behind the rubber and he throws to first. Many left-handed pitchers give their moves away with their heads. Generally they will look to home and throw to first, or look to first and throw home. A good baserunner or coach will pick up on this and take advantage of it. Be sure to vary the way that you attempt to pick off a runner so that you do not become predictable.

Pickoffs at second are tougher to execute because they demand precise timing between the pitcher and middle infielders. The most common pickoff at second is referred to as the "day light " play. This is when the shortstop sneaks behind the runner to cover second. When the pitcher sees "day light" between the shortstop moving to second and the baserunner, he wheels and throws to second base. The shortstop can call for the throw by extending his glove hand towards second. This sign also tells the pitcher that he is committed to going to second base. If the pitcher decides not to make the throw to second, he can step off the rubber so that his shortstop can get back to his position. A pitch should never be delivered home when an infielder is attempting a pickoff. This same type of play can be used by the second baseman, obviously without the day light segment. The second baseman should break for second and extend his bare hand letting the pitcher know when to throw the ball.

Another pickoff used at second base has the shortstop

holding the runner close by shortening up to the bag and making the runner aware that he is there. After doing this, he retreats to his normal position. At this moment the second baseman goes hard to the bag for the pickoff throw, again showing his hand to the pitcher. The play works with a very aggressive baserunner who will try to increase his lead when he sees the shortstop retreat.

A third pickoff at second involves the catcher. During his signs to the pitcher, the catcher may decide to put the pickoff sign on. This sign must be seen by the pitcher and the middle infielders. As the pitcher sees the pickoff sign, he must remember to check the runner on second as usual so that the runner does not become suspicious, and then look back to the catcher. The catcher watches the infielder (second baseman for a right-handed hitter, shortstop for a left-handed hitter). When the infielder breaks for second, the catcher drops his mitt. The pitcher wheels and throws to second when he sees the catcher drop the mitt. By drop the mitt, I mean that the catcher moves his mitt from the target position down toward the ground. This can be a very effective play with the bases loaded or with runners on second and third because the baserunner at second is not being held close in those situations.

A final way to execute a pickoff play at second also

involves timing. On this method, the pitcher checks the runner at second in his normal fashion. When the pitcher turns back to the catcher, the covering infielder waits until the back of the pitcher's head is pointed to second base. At this time, he breaks for second as the pitcher wheels to throw. This play is usually initiated by the infielder giving a sign to the pitcher and the pitcher answering the sign or vice versa.

Some pitchers have the ability to execute a type of pickoff to second that can be very effective. This is done by starting their leg kick as if to deliver the ball home but instead continuing back towards second base with their front leg. Often times the baserunner will increase his lead when he sees the pitcher lift his front leg. If this happens, the pitcher has a good chance to pick off the runner with this "step through" move.

Pickoff attempts at third base rarely occur at the high levels of baseball. Some teams will occasionally try a timed play that has the third baseman break for third when the pitcher (right-handed) lifts his leg as if to go home. Most successful pickoffs at third are the catcher throwing out a runner that has strayed too far off the bag after the pitch was delivered home. Good throwing catchers should have pickoff signs with all of the infielders to take advantage of his arm.

There are two special pickoff plays that deserve discussion. The first occurs with runners on first and third and a right-handed pitcher. The pitcher begins his leg kick but steps to third and fakes a throw to third, remembering that he cannot break the plane of the rubber during his leg kick. He must also disengage or come off the rubber with his back foot. After the fake, he turns to the runner at first to see what has developed. If the runner has broken for second, the pitcher may have an easy out there. With less than two outs, the middle infielders may have to execute the play as if the early steal was on. With two outs, try to get the runner on first before the runner on third has a chance to score. Usually the fake to third will drive the runner there back, so that his ability to get a good jump home is hindered in the event of a play on the runner at first.

The second special play is for a left-handed pitcher with runners on first and second, or the bases loaded. It can also be used with a slow runner on first only, where the first baseman is playing behind the runner. In these situations the first baseman should be playing behind the baserunner. His depth is normally determined by the number of outs, but for this play he should be back to about double-play depth or around ten feet behind the baseline. When the pitcher begins his leg kick, the first baseman breaks for first and the pitcher throws to the bag. This is a great play to get out of an inning. The sign for this play comes from the dugout to the first baseman and then is given to the pitcher by the first baseman. The pitcher should give a designated answer to the first baseman.

CHAPTER 4

PITCHING AND CATCHING

Without a doubt, the most important ingredient to a successful team is solid pitching. In this chapter, I will discuss the strategies involved in pitch selection and handling a pitching staff. Obviously, the catcher's role is vital to the success of a staff. He must be a dependable receiver in whom the pitchers have confidence. A good catcher can often times guide a pitcher through outings where he may not have his best stuff by calling a smart game and staying positive with his battery mate.

There are many factors involved in designing a pitching staff. These include the size of your roster, the number of games per week, the capabilities of the individual potential pitchers, inning restrictions, and the length of the games in your league. At the lower levels of the game, where roster sizes are limited, players often times play a position in addition to having pitching duties. If your team plays two to three games per week, you may only need four or five pitchers. These guys will probably be easy to identify at a young age because of their advanced ability or arm strength. At higher levels of the game where more games are played per week, a deeper staff is needed. Setting up this type of staff involves more planning as to starters and relievers. Regardless of the age of the players, managers must always be careful not to overwork certain pitchers. This is a real concern when dealing with young boys whose arms are not fully developed. The temptation arises to throw your stud pitcher too much in an attempt to win as many games as you can, but this type of managing can not only injure that particular pitcher but also stunt the development of other pitchers on the team. Ideally, a pitching staff should be comprised of both right-handers and left-handers. This gives the manager some flexibility in attacking certain lineups. Personally, I love staffs with a lot of left-handed pitching. For some reason hitters at all levels seem to have more difficulty hitting left-handed pitching. I believe the reason for this is that hitters see far more right-handed pitching as they are growing up and therefore become more comfortable facing righties. Also, left-handed pitching can often slow down an opponents base stealing game more effectively than right-handers can.

Some very basic common sense rules apply to all pitching. Statistics show that hitters perform significantly better when they are ahead in the count. Therefore, a pitcher's goal should always be to stay ahead in the count. First-pitch strikes are of vital importance to the success of any pitcher. As a pitcher, you should remember that the odds are stacked in your favor. The hitter does not know what type of pitch you are going to throw nor does he know where you are going to throw it. By throwing strike one on the first pitch you have immediately put him in a defensive frame of mind. His approach now is one that involves guesswork as opposed to being able to "sit" or wait on a certain pitch. Statistics also show that very few hitters are good first-ball hitters, especially the first time through the lineup. This is because they have no previous pitches to get their timing on. Also keep in mind that a mistake does not always end up as a basehit. Hitters will miss-hit mistake pitches or they may hit them right at someone for an out. To take the first pitch strike scenario further, breaking balls or off-speed pitches thrown for first pitch strikes can really mess with the mind of a hitter. Since most hitters would rather hit the fastball, a first-pitch strike with something other than a fastball serves two purposes. First, it plants the seed in their minds that you can throw that particular pitch for a strike. Second, they still have not seen your fastball, so their timing mechanism for the fastball is unknown.

A common mistake that I see with pitchers at the

lower levels of the game is that they pitch all hitters basically the same way. Remember that lineups are set up so that the better hitters are usually at the top and middle of the order. Each team has one or two extremely dangerous hitters surrounded by hitters of less ability. Extreme caution must be used when pitching to the hitters that can hurt you the most. For example, a pitcher who always throws a first-pitch fastball, regardless of who the hitter is, is taking a big chance because the hitters can now predict what pitch they will see. Many young pitchers set the pattern of throwing fastballs to get ahead and then breaking balls. This is a pitching sequence that hitters see most often, so they are used to this pattern and can pick it up quickly. This is an area where the catcher can really help the pitcher think through his pitch selection. Managers can also call pitches so that these predictable patterns are kept to a minimum.

The key to successful pitching is to keep the hitter off balance. This is accomplished by working ahead in the count as discussed earlier and by changing speed and location. All pitchers should try to develop a reliable off-speed pitch. The "circle change" seems to be the off-speed pitch of choice these days among successful hurlers. This pitch is thrown by making a circle with the thumb and forefinger and placing that circle along the side of the ball. The other three fingers are placed over the top of the ball, usually across the seams. The pitch is thrown with the arm speed of a fastball but because of the altered grip, the pitch does not travel as fast, thus deceiving the hitter. Other effective off-speed pitches include the forkball or split-fingered fastball, the palmball, and the knuckleball. These pitches are harder to master than the circle change. Pitchers that can throw off-speed pitches at any time in the count have a tremendous advantage over the hitter.

Location, or where you throw the pitch, is probably the single most important factor for pitchers to consider. Sure, everyone likes the guys who can throw 95 MPH and blow hitters away. But even those hard throwers had better throw their fastball in good spots or good hitters will catch up to them, especially at the higher levels of the game. A perfect example of a pitcher who masters hitters with excellent location is Greg Maddux. His ability to move the ball in and away from hitters has made him one of the best of all time. Understanding when to come inside to a hitter is crucial to a pitcher, and make no mistake about it, to be successful a pitcher must pitch inside. The reason for this is that all hitters like to get their arms extended when they swing the bat so that they can get the head of the bat through the strike zone. The length of the bat plus the length of the hitter's arms takes the head of the bat out over the plate and even to the outside corner. Inside fastballs are difficult for hitters to hit because they must commit to the swing a bit sooner in order to catch up to the pitch. That is why pitchers who pound hitters inside with hard stuff often times get hitters to swing at bad pitches. The hitter is aware that he must start his swing sooner so he is giving himself less time to identify whether or not the pitch is a strike or a ball.

Once a pitcher has established that he is not afraid to come inside, he now has control of the outside part of the plate as well. Obviously, if a hitter is protecting against the inside pitch, he cannot effectively handle the outside corner. This is why it is so important for pitchers to work both sides of the plate. The term "setting a hitter up" is what smart pitchers try to accomplish. The object is to try to induce the hitter into looking for a certain pitch and location and then crossing him up by throwing something else. This all sounds fairly simple and probably would be if all pitchers could throw the ball exactly where they wanted to on every pitch. Good hitters make the most of mistake pitches and this is what makes the battle exciting.

Pitchers also need to understand the situation of the game and what the hitter is trying to accomplish in a particular at bat in order to attack him most effectively. For example, if a left-handed batter is up with a man on second and no outs, his objective should be to pull the ball in order to advance the baserunner at least to third base. In this scenario the pitcher would be unwise to give the hitter pitches that he can easily pull, such as breaking balls or mediocre fastballs inside. Another example is if there is a good first ball, fastball hitter at the plate. Some pitchers will never give this type of hitter a fastball on the first pitch. This thinking is fine if you have good command of other pitches to get ahead of him with something other than a fastball. Other pitchers like to go after these types of aggressive hitters by trying to entice them into swinging at a fastball in a difficult location. In other words, if you are fairly certain that a hitter will offer at any first-pitch fastball because of his past history, then it would be foolish to groove one for him to swing at. A fastball off the plate will probably get you ahead of this type of hitter because of his aggressive style.

As discussed earlier in the chapter, getting ahead and controlling the count are of utmost importance. When hitters are behind in the count, they become much less disciplined than when they are ahead. A disease called "two-strike anxiety" afflicts many hitters, even major leaguers. This is apparent when you see hitters who are ordinarily fairly disciplined at the plate swing at bad balls with two strikes. The fear of striking out induces them to expand their strike zone to the point of swinging at anything remotely close to the plate and in some cases to swinging at pitches not close at all. Because of this defensive approach when behind or with two strikes, pitchers need to learn how to take advantage of the situation. I feel that a hitter is more vulnerable inside when behind in the count because he is trying to protect the whole plate, which is very difficult to do. Always keep track of what types of pitches the hitter likes and dislikes, and know the tendencies of as many hitters as you can. This can be done by making mental notes as you face certain hitters or by actually keeping a book on hitters, recording the situations that you faced them in and what kind of success that you had with them.

The pitcher-catcher relationship is very important in this whole scenario. A catcher must be aware of his pitcher's strengths and weaknesses in order to call a smart game. Generally, I would recommend that catcher's call the game according to the particular strengths of his pitcher rather than to the weaknesses of the hitter. For example, a pitcher with a good live fastball should not be afraid to throw his fastball to a good fastball hitter. Again, location is the key in all pitch selection. Some pitchers will throw whatever the catcher calls for, while others prefer to call their own game. A catcher's job is to handle the pitcher by making him as comfortable as possible while he is on the mound and also between innings. Talk about the hitters and develop a game plan of attacking them that both of you feel confident about. Catchers also need to gain their pitcher's trust in his ability to block balls in the dirt. This is an area of a catcher's game that often gets overlooked, but is of vital importance. A common mistake that catchers make when trying to block balls is that they try to "pick" or catch the ball in the dirt rather than block or "smother" it. Proper technique is for the catcher to collapse onto his knees while leaning forward with his chest in an effort to knock the ball down or smother it in front of him. This can prevent a wild pitch that may result in another run scoring opportunity for the opposition.

Another skill that catchers must develop is the art of framing pitches. This is the ability to catch border-line pitches smoothly so that the umpire has the illusion that the pitch was a strike. To do this effectively, a catcher must master certain skills. First, on border-line low pitches, the catcher should attempt to receive the ball with the fingers of his glove pointing down so that he can more easily move the ball back toward the bottom of the strike zone. This "pulling" the pitch up will give the umpire the idea that the pitch is not as low as he originally thought. If low pitches are caught with the palm down, the natural catching motion will take the ball away from the bottom of the zone and most times result in a "ball" call. Second, framing pitches on the corners is also very important. This skill starts with the catcher's set-up position. If the catcher has called for an outside pitch, then he should set up so that the middle of his body is on the outside corner. This serves two purposes. First, it gives the pitcher a better target to throw to and second, if the pitch is a little outside of the target the catcher does not have as far to reach for the ball and can sometimes pull the pitch back to the corner and get a favorable call. Another trick that catchers use is to position the glove just off the plate (inside or outside) so that when they catch a pitch a couple of inches off the plate their glove is not moving and the umpire sees this and calls a strike. Catchers must be careful not to set up too soon on either corner as observant opposition may see this and tip off the hitter as to the location of the pitch.

Another part of pitching that I would like to touch on has to do with the proper mechanics of the pitching motion. Obviously, there are many successful pitchers who have developed their own style as far as their methods of wind-up and delivery. However, I feel that certain basic fundamentals can be taught to young pitchers (and even older pitchers who may be experiencing problems) to get them into the correct position to deliver the ball home. First in the line of progression is the set-up position for a full wind-up. (This discussion will pertain to right-handed pitchers. Left-handers would set up just the opposite). When setting up on the rubber to take the sign from the catcher, the pitcher should have his right foot placed over the front edge of the rubber so that the ball of his foot is even with the leading edge of the rubber. A common mistake with young pitchers is that they place their foot on top of the rubber and stay on top throughout their wind-up. As the pitcher faces the catcher, I would recommend that he be turned slightly to his right (toward the third base dugout) with his glove hand placed in a fingers up position about eight to ten inches out in front of his chest. His throwing hand should be gripping the ball in the glove. The reason for the slightly turned starting position is that it is much easier to get to the final throwing position from this point. The pitcher starts his delivery by stepping back with his left foot at the same angle back that his shoulders are pointing forward. In other words, his step back would be towards right-center field. As he steps back to begin his motion, his hands remain in front of his chest. After the step back, the next move is the swinging of the left leg forward and up into a cocked position. Just before the left leg swings through, the right foot must turn clockwise so that the entire foot is now in front and parallel to the rubber. The final wind-up position should be a balanced one with the left knee up to the chest area and the glove still out in front of the pitcher. To deliver the ball home, the pitcher merely glides toward home with his left leg. A common teaching mistake is to tell the pitcher to drive toward home by pushing off his back foot. This method encourages the pitcher to accelerate his motion and often times he cannot get his arm in a position to throw the ball quickly enough, resulting in control problems. As the gliding to home begins, the pitcher removes the ball from the glove and takes it back in a circular long-arm method to the point where he releases the pitch from. As the front foot touches the ground, the throwing arm should be in position to release the ball. The ideal position for the lead arm (left arm) is a bent elbow with the fingers of the glove pointing up. This lead arm should feel as though it is pulling the upper torso through the rotation of the trunk just before delivery. The follow through should be a natural following of the right leg over the left, pivoting foot and into a good fielding position. Once the pitcher releases the ball, he becomes an infielder and must be ready to make a play.

There are many drills that a pitcher can practice to become adept at his skill. Perhaps the simplest advise, though is to throw a lot to develop arm strength. Long toss is one of the best drills to increase arm strength. Another good drill is to have the pitcher begin his wind-up and progress to the point where his left leg is in the cocked position (knee up in front of the chest). At this point have him stop and balance on his right foot. Mastering this balanced turn is critical for all pitchers. A third drill is to have the pitchers throw to a catcher at half the normal pitching distance for their level. This encourages them to develop a release point out in front of their body that will result in a pitch down in the strike zone. As they experience success in throwing strikes from this range, they can move back a few steps and repeat the drill until they are finally back to the normal distance.

The last item that I would like to mention about pitching is the skill of throwing to a specific target. Many accomplished pitchers at the highest levels of the game focus their concentration on throwing to spots or targets in the strike zone or even out of the strike zone depending on the count. I believe that throwing to a specific, small target as opposed to throwing to a large area is essential to developing pinpoint control. To execute this, a pitcher must focus on a particular target such as the catcher's glove or his knee, etc. This type of mentality will encourage the pitcher to recognize the different release points that he must have in order to put the ball where he wants it. By blocking out all outside distractions and focusing only on the target, the pitcher can eliminate the anxiety involved with facing tough situations. Many major league pitchers claim that they do not even see the hitter but rather focus only on their target. This level of concentration is obviously very difficult to attain, but any strides toward this goal will benefit the aspiring pitcher.

Set-up position. Back pointed to right-center, right foot over front of rubber.

Diagonal step back.

Midpoint of delivery. Notice right foot has pivoted in front
of rubber. Hips are closed, preparing to glide toward home.

Glide home. Left arm in "pulling through" position.

Follow through. Notice how the left arm has pulled the rotation of the upper torso around.

Stretch position with basestealer on first. Notice wide base and hands held high.

Slide step. From wide base, take a quick step towards home.

Circle-Change Grip.

Catcher setup in basestealing situation. Notice right foot (pivot foot) slightly behind left foot. Crouch is slightly higher than normal.

Catcher's throwing position. Notice right foot remains in the same spot for a quick pivot. Left foot steps to target. Short-arm throwing technique.

Catcher's blocking ball technique. Notice down on knees. Upper torso slanted forward to smother ball and keep it in front. Hands attempt to block, not catch, the ball.

CHAPTER 5

HITTING

Perhaps the most difficult skill to master in all of sports is that of hitting a baseball. The reason for this is that a hitter may do everything mechanically correct in a particular at bat and still make an out because he hit the ball right at someone or the defense made a great play on him. Because of this, hitters must develop a mental toughness that enables them to measure the success of their at bats in other ways than what the actual result of the at bat was. In other words, some great at bats result in an out, so the hitter must recognize that he accomplished something positive in the at bat even though he made an out. This way of thinking will prevent the hitter from getting down on himself and enable him to remain confident for the ensuing at bats. Hitters must remember that the greatest hitters of all time are successful in terms of getting basehits only 30% of the time or three out of every ten at bats. That means that they are making seven outs for every three hits. How a hitter deals with the outs that he makes is crucial to his future success as a hitter. That is why it is important to measure at bats in other ways, such as patience at the plate, not swinging at bad pitches, moving runners along, hard contact, etc. As you can see, an at bat can be deemed successful in many ways other than whether or not it resulted in a base hit. My goal as a hitter was simple - hit the ball hard. By keeping things that simple I found that I could eliminate much of the stress involved in worrying about the results of each at bat.

I feel that the most important aspect of successful hitting is having a good knowledge or command of the strike zone. Many hitters struggle mainly because they swing at bad pitches. The art of knowing the strike zone begins with batting practice. Good hitters show discipline during their practice time by swinging at strikes only. This develops the good habits that a hitter needs to take into the game. A good method of learning the strike zone is to have the hitter take the first four or five pitches during batting practice and call out whether he feels the pitch was a ball or a strike. This encourages him to identify the pitch first and should provide him with a better idea of his particular zone. By working on this skill of identifying balls and strikes the hitter is developing confidence in his ability to trust his judgement during the game.

Obviously, great hitters of all eras have batting styles that are unique to their own particular strengths or weaknesses. There is no magical stance or style that can be taught to hitters as "THE WAY" to hit. However, when watching great hitters, there are some common denominators present that enable them to achieve the success that they have. I will mention these in no particular order of importance, because they all are essential in and of themselves. By understanding and mastering these skills, hitters of all ages can improve their chances of success.

I am sure that anyone who has ever played the game has heard at one time or another the phrase "keep your eye on the ball". While this is good advice, it can also be confusing to hitters because they all believe that they are seeing the ball. I like to use the words "take your nose to the ball" in place of keep your eye on the ball because I feel that this encourages the hitter to keep his head in the proper position throughout the swing. If a hitter's nose is pointing at the ball during his swing, than his eyes must also be on the ball. When observing great hitters you will see that their heads actually go down towards the ball as they begin their swing. This head down position is crucial. Another point worth mentioning about the hitter's head and eyes is this. Face the pitcher in a way so that your head and eyes are level, not tilted. We do not normally walk around and view things with our heads tilted, so why hit with a tilted head. Many hitters face the pitcher with their heads slightly tilted towards the plate in such a way that their back eye's view is actually obstructed by the bridge of their nose. This can be easily corrected by moving the head more upright and turning it toward the pitcher.

Another obvious common thread that all great hitters execute is a move that keeps their hands back as they stride into the pitch. This move is started by turning or closing the front shoulder toward the plate as the pitch is delivered. As the shoulder closes, the hands go back. As this process is taking place the hitter is identifying whether or not the pitch is to his liking and if so, he attacks the ball from there. I always recommend that hitters try to keep their hands at or near the top of the strike zone and swing down through the zone. This also gives the hitter a good reference point as to where the top of the strike is so that any incoming pitch above his hands he can take. Power hitters usually carry their hands a little lower in the zone so that they can employ a slight upper-cut swing to drive the ball in the air.

This move of closing the front shoulder to get the hands back provides the hitter with the best chance to maximize his power. It also creates a rhythm during the swing that is important for increasing bat speed through the strike zone. The opposite move to closing the front shoulder is obviously to open it. Opening the front shoulder, or rotating it to the left (for a right-handed hitter), brings the hands forward. To illustrate this to yourself, stand as though you are holding a bat in a normal right-handed batting stance. Now simply rotate your left shoulder to the left and you will notice that your hands move forward in response to the shoulder movement. Conversely, if you rotate the left shoulder to the right, your hands will move back. Hitters that are struggling will usually have some degree of opening of the front shoulder taking place as they stride. This move causes their heads to move away from the plate as well as their hands coming forward. A great drill to practice the feel of closing the front shoulder is to have a partner toss balls underhand to the hitter from a spot about six feet in front and off to the side that the hitter is facing. The hitter can practice the closing of the shoulder and swing at the soft-toss and hit it into a screen or net. A batting tee could also be used for this drill.

The next topic worth mentioning about successful hitters is how they grip the bat. Very few, if any, great hitters choke the bat. By this I mean, grip the bat way back in their thumb joint. This grip tightens the muscles of the wrist and hands and prevents the hitter from making a quick, fluid swing. The correct grip technique has the bat laying out on the fingers, thus relaxing the wrist and hand muscles, and increasing the capabilities of making a faster more powerful swing. There is a hitting device on the market called "Direct Protect" that promotes the proper grip technique. This device is a small oval shaped pad that fits over the thumb of the top hand of the hitter. The pad rests in the thumb joint area, so that when the hitter grips the bat he cannot possibly choke the bat because the thickness of the pad keeps the bat out on his fingers. This pad also protects the thumb joint from bruising due to getting jammed. Amazingly, there are currently about 30% of the major league players using this device.

Many young hitters worry about their stance too much. All the beginning stance of a hitter should provide is a comfortable starting point from which to begin his swing. Hitters are successful using many different types of stances, so obviously there is no correct stance to teach. I recommend a comfortable, relaxed starting point that enables the hitter to execute the fundamentals of the swing that I have discussed previously such as head position, shoulder turn etc. Position in the batter's box is something that can greatly enhance a hitter's chances for success. For example, a hitter who likes the ball inside should crowd the plate, or move closer to the plate. This gives him the advantage of seeing pitches out over the plate as inside, which he likes. Conversely, a hitter who likes the ball away should move away from the plate.

Most good hitters stride into the pitch in a gliding rather than jumping move. Some sound advice that helped me during my career was "slow feet, quick hands". All this means is simply take a controlled stride and fire the hands through the zone. A hitter's stride must promote the shoulder turn and head down mechanics that I discussed earlier. This is more easily achieved through a deliberate gliding move into the pitch. As the hitter strides and begins his swing, his weight should transfer from his back side to his front leg. Many young hitters have a very difficult time with this weight transfer concept. Their mistake is to end up in a rather awkward reverse pivot, where they are actually leaning back as they swing. Their weight shift starts forward but then goes back as they swing the bat. To correct this, have the player swing the bat and drag his back toe forward as he completes his swing. This encourages the weight shift to complete itself onto the front foot because the back foot cannot support any weight while dragging forward.

A hitter's ability to use the whole field is also crucial to his success. Hitters who limit themselves to pulling the ball are easy to defend and easier to pitch to. Since the angle of the bat at impact determines where the ball will go, hitters need to work on manipulating the bat through the strike zone, creating different bat angles to see what it takes for them to hit the ball the other way or up the middle. To hit the ball the other way, or to the opposite field, the hitter must create a swing that leads with the hands and lets the head of the bat trail through the zone. This type of contact will have the head of the bat pointing toward the first-base dugout (for a right-handed hitter) at the moment of contact. Hitters need to work on these skills of bat manipulation during every batting practice to get a feel for handling the bat. As with bunting, if the head of the bat is above the hands at contact, the result will be a ground ball or line drive, usually the desired result when hitting the other way.

At this time, I would like to speak to the mental approach of hitting. As mentioned earlier, it is very important to stay as positive as possible for every at bat. Having a sound approach to your at bats means being prepared to execute whatever the situation calls for. We used to use the phrase "have an idea" to encourage fellow players to go to the plate with a plan of attack in mind. As with so many things in sports, hitting is as much mental discipline as anything else. I played with many great hitters in my career and learned what it was that made them successful. Hitters are always looking for something that will give them a mental edge at the plate. I have found that what hitters do between at bats or between games is often what gets them focused for the actual game at bats. These activities include watching video of their at bats, doing strengthening exercises for their hands and forearms, structured purposeful batting practice, and the ability to relax. Going to the plate knowing that you are prepared both physically and mentally should put the hitter in a confident frame of mind, ready to get the job done. The difficult part about hitting is trying to stay positive when dealing with making outs. That is why it is important to try to take something positive away from every at bat.

So what should a hitter be thinking when he goes to the plate? The particular situation dictates what he desires the result of the at bat to be. For example, there are definite times to try to advance base runners with a ground ball to the right side. There are times when a fly ball is needed to drive a run home from third. I could go on and on with different scenarios, but the point is that the hitter will always have an identifiable objective with each at bat. A coach or manager's job is to help players understand what the task is with each at bat. This should be done by going over every imaginable situation during practice sessions so that the hitters can become accustomed to recognizing what their goal is in the at bat. Some managers also have signs for different situations, such as a "get him over " sign with a man on second, to remind the hitters of what their job is.

Knowing the situation, the hitter now must go to the plate looking for a pitch that he can handle in order to get the job done. I received some advice from Ted Simmons, the fine switch-hitting catcher for the Cardinals in the 70's and early 80's, while I was a minor league player for the Cardinals. His advice was to always look for or expect the fastball, no matter what the count. The reasoning behind this is simple. As a hitter, you grow up seeing primarily fastballs in practice and your timing is based on reacting to fastballs. If you are expecting a fastball you will be ready to hit it in the event that you see one. If the pitch is not a fastball, say something off-speed, you can adjust to it accordingly. This is why keeping the hands back is so important. It is virtually impossible to hit the fastball if you are looking for an off-speed or breaking ball, because mentally you have geared your timing to slow down for the off-speed pitch. So the rule of thumb is "look for the fastball, react to the off-speed pitch". I'm sure you have seen hitters with two strikes on them just "lock up" and take a fastball down the middle for strike three. This was because they were guessing breaking ball and could not react to the fastball.

As mentioned earlier in the pitching chapter, the count is very important to both the pitcher and the hitter. Usually the count dictates what the pitch will most likely be. When the count favors the pitcher, he has more flexibility as to what type of pitch to throw next. Conversely, when the count is in the hitter's favor he can be more selective in what he is looking for as far as the type of pitch and its location. The best hitter's counts are 2-0 and 3-1, or 3-0 if the hitter has the "green light" or swing away sign. These are fastball counts and the hitter can really gear up for the fastball on these counts. I do not feel that hitters should guess what pitch is coming, but favorable counts make for educated guessing which is about as good as it gets for the hitter. There is a difference between looking for or being ready for a fastball and guessing. Guessing often times gets the hitter in trouble because he is totally committed to one pitch as opposed to being able to react to something else. I was a hitter who was comfortable hitting deep in the count so I often took pitches early in the count. This method of hitting served two purposes for me. One, it gave me a good reading on the velocity of the pitcher and two, I often saw a variety of pitches so that I knew what the pitcher had in his arsenal on that particular day. If the count worked in my favor then I was in one of those green light or educated guess situations that all hitters are more comfortable in. If the count worked in the pitcher's favor, at least I had a good gauge on his pitches and could battle him from there. Another thing that helped me when I fell behind in the count was to think "up the middle-the other way". This means that I was committed to hitting the ball to those areas of the field and it forced me to stay back and see the pitch before starting my swing. This thinking also helped me to take close pitches for balls, thus working the count back to my favor. Obviously, this approach to hitting means that the hitter must be willing to hit with two strikes on him, because often times this is what occurs. Again, a disciplined approach and a good command of the strike zone are essential to any approach and these areas should be stressed when preparing for game situations.

Grip on bat. Notice bat out in fingers of top hand.

Left-handed stance. Notice head level, both eyes can see
pitcher. Hands at top of strike zone.

Left-handed stride. Notice front shoulder closes to keep hands back. Hips are closed.

Left-handed swing. Notice nose to ball keeps head down. Weight has transferred to frontside, back foot drag. Hips have opened.

Left-handed reverse pivot. Common mistake caused by not completing weight transfer. Notice weight is transfered back to rear foot during swing.

Right-handed stance. Both eyes on pitcher. Hands at top
of strike zone.

Right-handed stride. Notice closed front shoulder keeps
hands back. Hips are closed.

Right-handed swing. Notice nose to ball keeps head down.
Weight transfers to front side, back foot drags.

Right-handed reverse pivot. Weight has shifted to back side during swing, caused by stiff front leg.

Sacrifice bunt. Head of bat above handle. Knees bent - ready to flex more on low pitch. Notice fingers of left hand are not wrapped around bat - this prevents injury on balls bunted at the label of bat.

Bunt for hit. Left foot steps through towards pitcher. Bat angle promotes ball hit on ground. Shoulders square.

Right-handed drag bunt. Bat angle promotes ground ball
to third base line.

CHAPTER 6

OFFENSE AND SITUATIONS

The object for any team on offense is to score more runs than the opponent. This can be done in many ways, by good hitting, using the running game, bad defense by the opponent, etc. In this chapter I will discuss various plays and the theory behind them as well as the proper technique in executing them. These plays include all aspects of the game from an offensive standpoint, with an emphasis on the responsibilities of the players involved, as well as strategically correct times to utilize these plays.

1. BUNTING FOR A BASEHIT - This is a ploy that must take the other team by surprise in order to have the highest chance for success. However, excellent bunters can still be successful even if the defense is wary of the bunt. The key to executing a bunt hit is to wait until the last possible fraction of a second before you show bunt. This is done by waiting until the pitch is on its way before bringing the bat through to bunt. As with all bunts, the object is to get the ball on the ground and close to the line, especially if bunting toward third. Creating the proper bat angle at the moment of contact is essential. A right-handed hitter needs to "cast" the head of the bat out in front of the plate, pointing the head towards the secondbase position. This casting is similar to the motion a fly fisherman would use to cast a fly. The right or top hand slides up the bat to a spot just below the label. Always remember that the head of the bat must stay above the handle to create a bunt that will go down. Another key is to make contact out in front of the plate. Left-handed batters should employ the same casting motion and can also step to the pitcher with their back foot as they make the casting move. Their bat angle should have the head of the bat pointing toward the third base dugout for a bunt to third base or toward the shortstop for a bunt between the pitcher and the firstbase line.

A player who has the ability to steal a base can bunt anytime, regardless of the outs. Non-basestealers should not bunt with two outs, as their objective is to try to get themselves into scoring position by hitting an extra basehit. Generally speaking, fastballs from the waist to the top of the strike zone and breaking balls are the easiest pitches to get down. The reason for this is that it is easier for the batter to maintain the proper bat angle, head above handle, on higher fastballs. Breaking balls are going down as they come into the plate and thus are easier to stay on top of if the bat angle is correct. When facing a left-handed pitcher, a good tactic is to try to push a bunt past him towards the second baseman, as the lefty pitcher usually falls toward third base on his follow through. The manager should have a "bunt for a hit" sign for situations that a baserunner is needed. These would include any time he sees that the corners are back or appear to not be expecting a bunt or when his team needs to get the tying or winning run to the plate.

2. SACRIFICE BUNT - This play is used to advance a baserunner one base. The batter must realize that he is giving himself up by bunting in order to move the runner. He should not try to disguise the sacrifice and bunt for a hit. The proper time to square around is just when the pitcher lifts his leg to start his delivery from his set position. Hitters from both sides of the plate should step toward the pitcher with their back foot so that it ends up a little in front of the other foot. A good trick is to move up in the batter's box so that when you square around your bat is well out into fair territory. Slightly bend the knees and create the head above handle bat angle. Bunt strikes only! Many times the squaring around of the batter will distract the pitcher, causing him to aim the ball or let up and miss the zone.

When attempting to bunt a man from first to second, the hitter should try to place the bunt somewhere between the pitcher's mound and the first base line. Do not jab at the ball as it is coming in, but rather create the feel of cradling or catching the ball with the head of the bat. This action will deaden the bunt and get the job done. When attempting to bunt a runner to third, the bunt should force the third baseman to come in to field it, thus leaving third base unoccupied. A firmer grip with the top hand will cause the ball to come off the bat harder to get it by the pitcher. With runners on first and second, the hitter should try to deaden the ball as close to the line as possible to thwart a possible rotation play that the defense may have on where the shortstop covers third for the force out.

A baserunner's responsibilities are equally as important as the bunter's. From his normal lead, the runner must take two to three lateral hop steps toward the next base as the pitch is being delivered. Be careful not to be leaning or off balance in case the batter misses or takes the pitch. Read the bunt off the bat. If the ball comes down off the bat, take off; if the ball is popped up, retreat. It is also a good practice to watch the play unfold as you are running to the next base so that you can determine whether or not a slide is needed. Contrary to popular belief, this does not slow the runner down.

There are really no set rules that dictate when a manager should bunt. Bunting a man to second can be done with no one out or with one out. Bunting a man to third should only be done with no outs, so that a sacrifice fly or ground ball out can score the man from third. An exception to this would be with runners on first and second and one out in a situation where a double play would prevent the heart of the lineup from coming to the plate in a crucial situation.

3. RUN AND BUNT PLAY - This play is a variation of the sacrifice bunt where the object of the play is to move the baserunner from first to third on the bunt. The play starts with the baserunner taking his lead and breaking for second on the pitch as if stealing the base. The duty of the batter is to square around as the pitcher lifts his front leg, just like the normal sacrificing technique. The batter must bunt the ball down the third base line so that the charging third baseman must field the ball. To execute this, the batter must create the proper bat angle; that is, the head of the bat should be pointing at the second baseman (for right-handed hitter). Grip the bat firmly with the top hand so that the ball will come off the bat harder. At the moment that the bunt is rolling toward the third baseman, the baserunner should be at or near second base and continue on to third.

Obviously, this is a risky play and should be tried only in certain situations and with certain batter-runner combinations. The runner must be a player with basestealing-type speed and the hitter should be an above average bunter. The count on the hitter is also a factor when trying to pull off this play. Wait for the hitter to be ahead in the count so that the pitcher is in a situation where he must throw a strike. A good time to try this play is with no outs in the middle of the game to try to add to a lead. Proper execution will result in a man on third with one out where a fly ball or ground out may get you the insurance run. Another factor in this play is the strength of the first baseman's arm. This is a tough throw and one that the first baseman is not used to making, which makes the play harder to defend.

The run and bunt play can also be called with men on first and second when the manager feels that the defense might have the rotation play on. Starting the runners will allow the runner on second to beat the force at third.

4. SLUG BUNT - Another wrinkle in a sacrifice situation is the slug bunt. This play calls for the hitter to square around by rotating his upper torso and showing bunt. As the pitch approaches, the hitter brings his hands back into a hitting position and swings at the pitch, trying to hit a ground ball through the middle portions of the infield. What makes this technique successful is that the middle infielders often vacate their positions to cover a base when the hitter shows bunt, leaving large holes in the infield for the batter to punch a ground ball through.

This play should be called only when the opposing team is expecting a sacrifice so that they will "bite" on the bunt fake. Some managers also like to start the runner on this play and treat the play like a hit and run play, trying to get a first and third situation from it. In this case the hitter must swing at the pitch to protect the runner. If the play is called without the runner going, then the hitter can be more selective and only offer at strikes. Again, the types of hitters that can execute this play are limited to guys that can handle the bat and have the ability to stay on top and hit a ground ball. Spend some time practicing this technique to find out which players can execute.

5. SQUEEZE BUNT - Proper execution of the squeeze bunt can be almost impossible to defend. The object of the play is bunt a runner from third to home. The hitter's task is to get the bunt on the ground anywhere but directly back to the pitcher. The timing of the bunter is critical to the success of this play. Do not show bunt until the pitch has left the pitcher's hand. Concentrate on the proper bat angle (head of bat above handle) and bend the knees when squaring around to enable you to react to pitches out of the strike zone. Remember that you must try to bunt the pitch no matter where it is to protect the runner. The baserunner on third has an important job as well. Take a safe lead and be walking toward home plate as the pitcher begins his wind-up. Break for home when the pitcher's throwing arm starts to the plate, as at this point it is too late for him to alter his delivery. If the pitcher is throwing from the stretch, a slightly bigger lead should be taken because the walking technique will not be able to be used. Again, break for home when the pitcher's throwing arm starts for home.

When to use the squeeze is a question open for debate. Some managers do not like the play and rarely use it, others pick their spots. Generally speaking, I would not try the squeeze with no outs because the hitter's chances of plating the run are fairly good by swinging away. The element of surprise can make this play even more successful. For example, immediately after something disruptive has happened to the opposition is a good time to squeeze. The defense has a hard time regrouping from an adverse situation and may not be as mentally prepared for the squeeze. Other factors include the type of hitter, whether or not the infield is playing in, and the score of the game. Let me explain. A hitter that has trouble driving the ball would be a good candidate to squeeze, especially with the infield playing in, because his chances of hitting a sacrifice fly are slim and the drawn in infield could cut the run off at the plate on a ground ball. With the infield back, however, it is wise to let a ground ball hitter swing away, as the defense is conceding the run anyway and he may find a hole for a base hit and the potential for a bigger inning is there.

6. LEADS AND BASE STEALING - The most important factor in having an effective basestealing game is the quality of leads that baserunners take. This is an area of the game that often gets very little time in practice or is over looked all together. Basically there are two types of leads that should be taught to players. The first is the one way or safety lead. This is the type of lead that baserunners should take late in the game with your team trailing by two or more runs. The object of this lead is to not allow the baserunner to get picked off or doubled off on a line drive out. This lead should be no more than six feet off the bag and the runner is thinking only base to base or one base at a time. No chances are to be taken in this situation such as trying to go first to third or trying to advance on a ball blocked by the catcher. The manager should have a sign to the runner or first base coach to let the runner know that the one-way lead situation is in effect.

The other lead is called a two-way lead and as the name suggests, this lead enables the runner to be able to go two ways, back to the bag or to the next bag. The distance off the bag for the two-way lead varies from runner to runner depending on their ability to get back to the bag on a pickoff attempt. I am a firm believer in taking measured leads so that the runner knows exactly how far off the bag he is. A measured lead is very easy to perfect and should be practiced routinely so that players become comfortable taking their leads without looking back at the bag to see how far off they are. The proper way to take a measured lead is for the runner to place his left foot along the edge of the bag closest to the next base, always keeping his eyes on the pitcher. From this position he steps sideways with his right foot to a distance approximately just past shoulder width. For teens and adults this step is roughly three feet, for youngsters slightly shorter. Now the lead foot is three feet from the bag and the left foot should be brought out and placed directly beside the right foot. Never cross over! The process is then repeated until the lead desired is attained. For most runners a three step or nine foot lead should be a comfortable two-way lead. Remember that the left foot is the foot that is nine feet from the bag and the right foot is actually out to twelve feet. Aggressive baserunners can get off more than this with the maximum lead being a point from which you can safely dive back to the bag on a pickoff attempt. Runners should all be taking a two-way lead that forces them to dive back on a pickoff attempt. This tells you that you have your maximum lead, but still a safe lead. The dive back to first is executed by crossing the right foot over the left, planting the left hand on the ground and reaching for the left corner of the bag with the right hand. A good practice is also to turn the head away from the pitcher on the dive back so that a throw in the dirt cannot hit you in the face.

Practice taking measured leads with a pitcher on the mound so that you become comfortable with how far you can get off the bag. It might be a good idea to actually measure your side step to let you know exactly how far each step takes you away from the bag and thus how many steps you need to take to get out to the nine to twelve foot range.

Reading a pitcher's move is the key to successful base stealing. Once the baserunner has secured his lead he should be in a slightly crouched position with his hands out in front and a little wider than his knees. His weight should be evenly distributed on the balls of his feet, ready to go in either direction. The key or tip-off that the pitcher gives may be a subtle movement or may be an obvious thing to look for. This is why it is extremely important to watch the pitcher whenever men are on base so that you can determine what part of his body tips off his delivery to home plate or his move to first.

I feel that the first move a baserunner should make when stealing a base is a combination of a cross-over step with the left foot and a thrusting or punching motion with the left arm going across the front of the body toward the next base. Try to stay low and gradually come up out of the crouch after two or three steps, much like a sprinter stays low coming out of the starting blocks. Pump the arms aggressively to reach top speed as quickly as possible and don't be afraid to glance in to the plate after the third step to see what is going on at the plate. This enables the baserunner to get back in case the hitter swings and pops the ball up, or may allow him to avoid a slide if the pitch gets by the catcher. This quick glance does not slow the runner down, contrary to popular belief. To finish off the steal, the runner should attempt a quick pop-up slide by sliding on the outside of front part of the calf muscle and immediately pushing off that same leg to get back up into a standing position. This technique allows the runner to continue to the next base quickly if the throw gets by the covering infielder.

A significant effort should be made at each practice session to work on these fundamentals of the running game. The fear of taking an aggressive lead must be eliminated before a baserunner can hope to achieve his potential on the bases. Baserunners should practice getting leads off of both right- and left-handed pitchers to get the feel for common tendencies that pitchers have. For example, many left-handers tip off their pickoff move by looking to home plate while throwing to first. This should be the first thing that a baserunner should look for against a lefty. Whatever tip-off a pitcher gives must be the focal point of the baserunner. If you pick something up, share the information with the rest of your teammates so that this area can be exploited.

Another tactic that can be used to steal a base is the delayed steal. This is a good method for runners who do not possess great basestealing speed to perfect. A delayed steal is disguised by the baserunner taking his normal two to three hop steps toward second base as the pitch is delivered home. On the third step, he simply breaks for second to steal the base. The element of surprise will hopefully throw off the timing of the catcher and whichever middle infielder is covering second. The catcher tends to relax when the runner does not break for the steal right away, and many times the middle infielders are caught with their heads down when they see that the runner is not breaking with the pitch.

The final area of discussion for this segment is how to take normal two-way leads when the steal is not on. A common mistake that players at all levels make is to remain stationary as the pitch is delivered home. This mistake can cost the baserunner from beating a close force play at the next base, can keep him from advancing to the next base on a short-passed ball, or prevent him from taking an extra base on a base hit to the outfield. The proper technique for baserunners is to take three lateral hop steps toward the next base as the pitch is made. As the pitch crosses home plate, the baserunner should be positioned on both feet with his weight evenly distributed, ready to break in either direction. Never be leaning to the next base, as now you are vulnerable to a pickoff attempt from the catcher. These rules apply for leads off of both first and second base, but change slightly for a lead off of third base. A runner at third should take a lead of about nine feet to start. As the pitcher starts his wind-up, the runner should walk toward home plate by stepping first with his right foot in a right-left-right technique. As the pitch is crossing home plate, the runner is landing on his right foot (third step) and is ready to break in either direction. Remember to stay in foul territory during the lead and retreat to third on the line or just inside the foul line. This protects the runner from being called out on a line drive that may hit him. Retreating on the line or inside it limits the catcher's visibility as to how far off the bag you are and forces him to throw a pickoff attempt well inside the foul line.

7. FIRST AND THIRD DOUBLE STEAL - This is a play that is often hard for lower level players to defend, and thus is quite an effective play to have in your arsenal. At the major league level, this tactic is less common because of the strong, accurate throwing arms that big leaguers have. The runner on third has the toughest job on this play because he must read the catcher's throw before he can break for home. If he sees the throw to second come out of the catcher's hand high, he can break right away. If the throw comes out low, he must wait until it passes the pitcher before he can break. Obviously, the runner at third can take more liberties if his team already has a lead in the game and is trying to steal a run to build on that lead. In tight games, the defense will probably have some sort of play on to defend against this double steal or just concede the runner to second base.

A variation of the play has the runner on first leaving early, just as the pitcher starts his stretch in an attempt to induce a balk or in an attempt to get the pitcher to throw the ball to first or second. If the pitcher throws the ball to first, the baserunner on first should break for second to induce a throw there from the first baseman. When this throw is made, the runner on third breaks for home. If the pitcher runs at the runner on first or turns and throws to second, the runner on third should creep off and break for home on the next throw. These plays are all obviously very high risk and the offensive team must be either willing, or in a position in the game, to take this risk.

Another variation of this play occurs when a left-hander is on the mound, hence it is called the "Lefty play". As the left-hander comes to his set position in his stretch, the runner on third breaks for home. When the runner on first sees the runner on third break, he takes off for second or falls down-anything to greatly distract the pitcher into paying a great deal of attention to him. If the pitcher makes any kind of move to the runner on first, the man breaking from third will score easily.

8. HIT AND RUN PLAY - This is one of my personal favorite plays, only because as a hitter, I had the ability to handle the bat and find holes in the infield when baserunners were moving. Keep in mind that with a man on first, the first baseman is holding the runner on and thus creating a nice, natural hole in the infield for the hitter to shoot for. Left-handed batters should be looking for something to pull through the hole in this situation if no play is on. Typically, in a steal situation, the shortstop will cover second with a left-handed batter up and the second baseman will cover against a righty. This is not set in stone, but even at the major league level this holds true the majority of the time. What makes the hit and run play so effective is that, in addition to the hole left by the first baseman, the offense can create more holes in the infield by starting the runner on the hit and run play.

The baserunner on first must treat the hit and run play differently than a steal. Never get picked off on a hit and run play. Always take a good two-way lead, but make sure that the pitcher is going home before you break for second. Remember that the hitter must swing the bat so that you will be protected somewhat in the event that he swings and misses. This play is safest when facing a pitcher that is always around the plate and in situations where the count is in the hitter's favor, where a fastball is the most likely pitch (1-0, 2-0, 2-1, 3-1). The hitter's mindset should be to keep his hands at the top of the strike zone and swing down through the zone in an attempt to hit a hard ground ball. For some hitters this will be the best that they can achieve, but for those who can handle the bat in a manner that enables them to hit the ball to a specific area of the infield, many basehits will result from this play.

A right-handed batter, in most cases, will have the second baseman covering on the steal. If the second baseman vacates his position too early, the entire right side of the infield is now open for a ground ball to get through. This is why right-handers must learn to hit the ball the opposite way. My technique was to widen my stance, thus shortening my stride, and keeping my hands closer to my body during the swing. This enabled me to create the bat angle needed to inside-out any pitch to right field. This angle is created by leading the bat through the strike zone hands first, and at the moment of contact, the head of the bat is pointed towards the first base dugout. Inside pitches are actually easier to hit the other way and keep fair than outside pitches, so I also crowded the plate to make everything seem inside. Sometimes middle infielders will give away who is covering by cheating closer to the bag. If you can pick this up as a hitter, you now know where to attempt to hit the ball. If you are a right-handed hitter with very strong tendencies to hit the ball to the opposite field, chances are that the shortstop will cover on a steal attempt and you should make an effort to pull the ball in a hit and run situation.

Left-handed batters do not have as much guesswork in hit and run situations because the defense should rarely, if ever, have the second baseman cover on the steal. Why? Because then the entire right side or pull side of the infield would be open for the hitter and this is not too smart. A left-handed hitter who can pull the ball easily should, in my opinion, pull the ball on the hit and run play. He still has the hole at first to shoot for and it is easier to pull the ball on the ground than it is to hit it the other way on the ground. If, on the other hand, you can hit the ball the opposite way, then go ahead and take a shot at hitting it through the hole at short.

The same bat angle principles apply to the left-handed hitter.

Hitters must remember that they have to swing at the pitch, no matter where it is, to protect the baserunner. This is a green-light situation for the hitter because he knows that he can be very aggressive and swing hard at the pitch. If the count is in your favor, a fastball is probably coming. If the pitcher crosses you up with something off-speed, a swing and a miss will not kill your at bat, and chances are the baserunner will steal the base on the slower pitch.

Let's get back to the baserunner. As on a steal attempt, you should be looking in to the hitter on your third step to see what the result of the swing is. Any ground ball through the infield in front of you is an automatic first to third situation. On a ball hit behind you, pick up the third base coach to see what his instructions are. The batter should run aggressively to first on a base hit, watching the outfielder's throw. If the outfielder makes a play on the runner going to third, you may be able to continue on to second. As with the other special plays, practice time should be devoted to perfecting this great offensive weapon. Also, hitters should use their batting practice wisely, attempting to hit the ball to all fields so that they can do so when called upon in game situations.

9. BREAKING UP THE DOUBLE PLAY - This is an area of the game that probably does not seem like such a big deal, but believe me, as a middle infielder, I was acutely aware of the opposing players who had a reputation for coming into second base hard to break up two. Dave Parker would stand on first and yell at me and Ozzie, "I'm coming to get you!" Another player with a great ability to wreak havoc on middle infielders was Lonnie Smith. These guys, and many others who were adept at breaking up the double play, have a few tactics in common that help them. First of all, they enjoy trying to intimidate on the bases. This mentality can set the tone for your team and create an aggressiveness that spreads to all the baserunners. The key to effectively breaking up two is to start the slide late and aim for the point from where the shortstop or second baseman will make his throw to first. The rules state that a player attempting to break up a double play must slide close enough to the base so that he could potentially reach out and touch the bag. Certain umpires will give the baserunner a little latitude in their interpretation of this rule, but generally speaking, the runner should slide no more than three or four feet to either side of the bag. Going in high is also a good way to disrupt the middle infielder, as this usually causes the middle infielder to not be able to jump over the sliding baserunner. The simple goal is to do anything that will prevent the successful turning of the double play. This can be done in a number of ways, from knocking the middle infielder off his feet to causing an errant or delayed relay throw.

Good middle infielders rarely leave themselves vulnerable to being knocked down. This is accomplished by coming across the bag and getting into a position to throw the ball that is well away from the bag. Second basemen do this by getting to the bag early and placing their left foot on top of the bag. As the throw is coming to them, they step to the throw with their right foot so that their pivot actually takes place about three to five feet on the third base side of the bag. Obviously, the man trying to break up two must slide to that side of the bag if he wants to get a shot at this guy. Second basemen who try to turn it right on the bag are the easiest target, as the runner can merely slide right over the bag to get them. Shortstops are harder to get because they have the runner in front of them and can adjust easier based on where the runner is when they catch the ball. Basically, in order to break up two, the baserunner must be committed to going all out and trying to get a piece of the middle infielder. Even when not successful, you have sent them the message that your team is coming after them. This may force the middle infielders to adjust their double play positioning a little closer to the bag, thus giving up a little bit of range. It also forces them to hurry which may in itself cause a foul up when turning two.

Another situation that occurs with the double play in order is a ground ball directly at the second baseman where he tries to field the ball and tag out the runner going to second before throwing to first. Baserunners should be aware that this possibility exists and be anticipating what to do. If the second baseman steps into the baseline, it is perfectly legal for the runner to take him out by colliding with him or by sliding into his legs to avoid the tag. The other option is to retreat to first to avoid the tag. This forces the second baseman to make a decision. The right play for the second baseman to make is to run the baserunner back a few steps, then throw the ball to first to retire the batter and create a rundown situation with the baserunner between first and second. If this happens, the baserunner must be aware that he can escape the rundown by getting to second base or first base safely because he is no longer forced at second due to the out already recorded at first. In many cases, however, the second baseman does not think that fast and makes one of two mistakes. He either chases the runner back to first in an effort to tag him, or he throws the ball to first too soon. In the first scenario, the second baseman often has trouble completing the double play with a throw to first because of the time it took to tag the runner out, or because he is off balance after making the tag. In this case, the baserunner did his job by not allowing the double play. The other scenario has the second baseman throwing the ball to first too soon when he sees the runner stop, thus allowing the runner to reach second safely when the throw to first is made. The worst thing that a runner can do is to allow the second baseman to make a routine tag and throw for the double play. Do something to disrupt the play!

10. RUNDOWNS - Rundowns are important to discuss because there are a few simple tricks that baserunners can try to escape them. Generally speaking, the longer that you can stay in a rundown, the better your chances are of escaping it. The reason for this is quite clear. The more throws that it takes to get you, the more chances the defense has to mess up. A bad throw, a dropped throw, a late throw, all can occur at any time during the rundown. Also, the longer you stay hung up, the better the chance of other baserunners moving up a base.

In order to understand how to get out of a rundown,

it is important to know the proper way for the defense to execute a rundown. A defense should try to record an out with as few throws as possible. This is done by running hard at the baserunner with the ball in the throwing hand and held up for the recipient of the throw to see. Never fake throws by pumping the arm back and forth because this will also fool your team-mate. The ideal rundown has the defense running at the runner and tagging him out without a throw. Always try to run him back to the base that he started from. The reason for running hard at the runner is to force him to sprint in order to avoid being tagged out and making it difficult for him to stop quickly and change direction.

To escape a rundown, try to stay halfway between the two infielders if possible. Try to force throws and most importantly look for a defensive player near the baseline to run into. If you run into a defensive player who does not have the ball during a rundown, you should get an interference call on the defense and be awarded the next base. If you are about to be tagged out, try to knock the ball loose by colliding with the hand holding the ball, probably the throwing hand.

If there are multiple runners on base with less than two outs, say second and third, and the runner on third gets into a rundown between third and home, the runner on second should get to third base and stay there. If the runner on third is run back to third base, the trailing runner should remain at third base. The worst thing that occurs here is that your team will still have a runner on third. If there are two outs and a scenario like this arises, the runner on second should stay near second in case the runner on third can escape back to third safely. It is important to know the rules concerning two baserunners occupying the same base. If the original baserunner gets back to third safely, and the runner from second has also gone to third base, the base belongs to the original baserunner and the runner from second can be tagged out. If this happens with two outs, the runner who came from second should break back to second rather than just allow himself to be tagged out. Who knows, maybe the defense will throw the ball away and the runner on third can score.

If you are a runner on third, and a baserunner behind you gets into a rundown, you may decide to break for home sometime during the rundown. There are no set rules for this, but usually if you can break just as a throw is being made your chances are better. The inning-score-out situation should dictate if it is a good time to try this. Obviously, if your team already is leading, you may be able to take more chances to increase the lead. If there are no outs, it is wise to stay at third regardless of the score because if the rundown results in a out, you will still be on third with only one out and your chances of scoring are still good.

11. TAGGING UP ON FLY BALLS - Proper technique on plays that require a baserunner to tag up is very important. Obviously, the most frequent tag plays occur from second or third base. Occasionally, however, an opportunity will occur that enables a runner to tag up at first and go to second. I will discuss these situations first.

The normal routine for a baserunner on first when a fly ball is hit is to start for second base and read the outfielder. On balls that look as though they will be caught, this read usually takes place anywhere from halfway to three-quarters of the way to second. As the outfielder camps under the fly ball, the runner retreats to first. Sometimes, though, outfielders will continue to drift back on balls that you may read as catchable. These are outfielders that you can possibly take advantage of. It is very important to know the arm strength of the outfielders. A situation that has a weak armed outfielder moving away from the infield to make a catch is a green light for the baserunner. When you see an outfielder drifting away from second base on a ball that you are sure he is going to catch, retreat to first before the catch is made. When he makes the catch, you should already be tagging up and sprinting to second. As you are going to second you have to again read the outfielder to see how quickly he gathers himself to make the throw. You can always stop and go back to first if he recovers quickly and makes an accurate throw. Usually, though, you will be able to challenge him because of the difficulty in making a strong throw after making a catch moving away from the infield. Never tag up if there is any doubt in your mind if the catch is going to be made. If you are not sure whether or not the catch is going to be made, you should get as close to second base as possible to wait to see what happens. If the ball drops in, you can go to third easily from this position, and maybe even score. If the ball is caught, you can return to first. Sometimes runners go past second base thinking that a fly ball is going to drop in, only to see the outfielder make a great catch. If this happens, make sure to re-tag second on the way back to first.

When tagging up from second or third base, some general rules apply. The baserunner should always tag up in such a way as to be facing the outfielder so that he can get the best jump possible. This is done by placing the appropriate foot on the bag that enables the runner to view the outfielder easily. For example, a runner tagging up from second on a fly ball to left center should tag up with his right foot on the bag (his back to first base) so that he is facing the catch. As he is running to third base, the third-base coach should be directing him which way to slide to avoid the tag. When tagging up from third, the baserunner should place his left foot on the bag and watch the catch, in addition to listening to instructions from the coach. First of all, whenever a ball is hit into the air, the runner on third must be conditioned to break back to third to tag up. This prevents the situation where the runner is too far off the bag to tag up on questionable fly balls, usually line drives or hump back liners in front of the outfielders. Obviously, on deep fly balls where there is little or no chance to be thrown out at home, the runner should take care not to leave too soon. On balls where there will be a play at the plate, timing the break from third is crucial. A good trick to practice is to actually begin the push off just before the catch is made. By the time the foot actually leaves the bag, the catch will have been made. On-deck hitters should position themselves in view of the on-coming baserunner to direct his slide.

In game situations where preventing the run from

scoring is crucial, baserunners behind the runner tagging from third should also be tagging up to advance. In most cases the throw will not be cut off and the trailing runner(s) can move up a base. If the throw is cut off, he may still be able to beat the relay throw to get the trailing runner or he may have to stop and get in a rundown to trade an out for a run. This type of chance is good to take late in the game when your team really needs the run to score. Early in the game, the trailing runner should still tag up, but read the throw from the outfield. If the throw looks high (missing the cutoff man) you can continue to the next base.

12. FIRST AND THIRD TAG PLAY - This is a special play that can be used to steal a run on short to medium fly balls that a man would not ordinarily tag up on from third. The play is great because of the element of surprise that it has and also because of the difficulty in properly defending the play.

The ideal type of fly ball or pop fly to try this play on is one down the right- or left-field lines. Let's say a pop fly is lifted down the right-field line with runners on first and third and less than two outs. The right fielder and second baseman, and maybe even the first baseman, all converge on the ball. Both baserunners should tag up and when the catch is made, regardless of who catches it, the runner on first should break for second. If he draws a throw to second base, the runner on third should break for home and will score easily. The dilemma for the player making the catch is where to throw the ball. If he throws to second, which he will usually do because he is surprised to see the runner break, the runner on third scores as I stated before. If he throws home, the runner on first will advance to second. The key to executing this play successfully is the runner on third not breaking for home until he sees the throw made to second. He should tag up and then walk off third, about one-third of the way to home to read what is going on. Another key to the play is trying it when there is no one in a cutoff position for the throw to second base- that is on balls that both the outfielder and middle infielders go for. A throw that travels the whole way to second without being cut off will be easy to score on. Even if there is a cutoff man, the play can work because it would take a good first and second throw to nail the man at the plate. If the play is attempted when the caught fly ball is the second out, the runner going to second base should not run into the out at second, but rather get into a rundown to allow the runner on third to score. This is a fun play and one that can really disrupt the opposition. Good times to try this play are when your team is trying to add to a lead, but are not limited to these situations because of the difficulty of defending the play. It is probably a good idea to have a sign to tell the baserunners to be alive to the possibility of the play coming up. An alert first base coach is important also because he can start the play on his own when he sees a pop-fly that fits the play.

13. GENERAL BASERUNNING RULES - The toughest thing about baserunning is knowing when are good or smart times to try to take the extra base. Aggressiveness is extremely important on the bases but running smart is equally if not more important. Many times, offenses will run themselves out of innings because of making poor decisions on when to try to take extra bases. Keep the following rules in mind when running the bases or coaching the bases: **Don't make the first or third out at third base.** This rule should be easy to understand. A runner is unwise to be thrown out at third with no outs because his chances of eventually scoring from second with no outs are fairly good. The next batter could advance him to third in numerous ways where he would then be with one out, or the batter could drive him in from second with a hit. Making the third out at third is also stupid for this same reason. You are already in scoring position at second

141

base so why risk ending the inning by going to third when it will take a hit to score you anyway. **Don't make the first or second out at home.** It doesn't make a lot of sense to get thrown out at home with no outs because of the high likelihood that you will score from third eventually. Making the second out at home is also ill-advised because a fly ball or ground-out can score you from third with one out.

These rules seem to imply that I am advocating a non-aggressive approach to baserunning, which isn't the case. As I said before, you can be both aggressive and smart when running the bases or coaching the bases. Obviously, the game situations that are present will dictate how aggressive you can be. When your team is trailing by two or more runs late in the game, you should be thinking base to base and not be willing to take too many chances. In situations where you can afford to take some chances, these rules are still helpful in dictating when or if you should try to advance. Another important aspect to keep in mind is the way that the outfielders are fielding the ball. Any ball that forces an outfielder to move laterally to retrieve is probably a good one to take a chance on, whereas, a ball that he can field moving in toward the infield is easier for him to throw because his momentum is helping him to execute the throw. Knowing the strength of the outfielders' arms is also important. To better equip yourself mentally, always watch the outfielders throw in pre-game to evaluate their strengths or weaknesses.

14. THE COURAGE PLAY - This is a seldom-used play because of the high risk involved in pulling it off. Basically, the courage play is a hit and run play with a runner on third. The play is called to attempt to score a run from third with less than two outs when the defense has the infield pulled in to prevent the run from scoring on a ground ball. The runner on third breaks for home when the pitch is released from the pitcher's hand. The batter's job is to hit a ground ball. Sounds simple enough, doesn't it? Obviously, the right type of hitter must be at the plate. This is a player in whom the manager has a great deal of confidence, one who is able to stay on top of any pitch to hit a ground ball. The play is a lot like the squeeze play, except that the offense is not sacrificing an out as in the squeeze. Sometimes the ground ball will get through a drawn in infield and create another run-scoring situation. Again this play is probably best used when trying to build upon a lead.

15. THE TAKE SIGN - Part of becoming a good hitter, oddly enough, is knowing when not to swing the bat. I firmly believe that there are times when the hitter should force the pitcher to throw a strike before he swings at a pitch. Often times, this will be dictated by the manager or coach, but other times, a hitter can take on his own to enhance his chances in that particular at bat. The type of hitter that you are has a lot to do with how often you should take pitches. By this I mean are you a hitter that "sets the table" or are you a hitter that drives in runs. I had a year in the minor leagues when I was the lead-off man for my team. I decided that my main job was to get on base for the big boys to drive me in. My approach that year was to automatically take a pitch on every 2-0 and 3-1 count. My thinking was that even if the pitcher threw a strike, I would still be ahead in the count and the chances of still getting a fastball on the next pitch were pretty good. As a result of this approach, I had one of my most productive years in the minors in terms of batting average, bases on balls, stolen bases, and runs scored. Later in my major league career when I became more of a run producer, I would swing away on those counts if RBI opportunities existed. The point is, taking pitches can greatly enhance a hitter's chances because of getting into favorable ball-strike counts.

Let's discuss when are good times to take a pitch. Many studies have been done to illustrate hitter's

144

averages on various counts. Most hitters, with very few exceptions, have far more success when they are ahead in the count. Also, very few hitters are good first-ball hitters, especially in their first at bat of the game. This is a fact that seems hard to understand since so many pitchers throw a first-ball fastball to try to get ahead in the count. I believe that hitters that are successful swinging at the first pitch they see are "zone" hitters. That is, they are looking for a particular location in addition to looking for the fastball. If a hitter has the ability to swing only at pitches in that zone, than this is a sound approach. Many hitters, though, swing at any first-pitch fastball regardless of where it is, and this is not a good approach. These types of hitters would be better off taking the first pitch and getting a feel for the pitcher's velocity and release point. The fear of having to hit the breaking ball often causes a hitter to be over aggressive on the first pitch of his at bat. He feels that if he takes a fastball strike, then he will get a breaking ball on the next pitch. This may indeed occur, but think of the situation this way. Breaking balls are usually harder for pitchers to throw for strikes, so there is no guarantee that the second pitch, if it is a breaking ball, will even be thrown for a strike. My main point is, that in order to get yourself into favorable count situations, you must be willing to take some pitches. Sometimes it is good to pre-plan your approach for the particular at bat so that you can go to the plate with an idea of how you want to carry out the at bat. You may tell yourself to take until you get a strike. This is a sound way to approach at bats because often times you will get yourself in good count situations by doing this. This is also a good approach for table-setter type hitters who have the ability to steal a base.

Other factors may also dictate when is a good time to take a pitch. If you notice that a pitcher is having a hard time throwing strikes, either during his warm ups or to a previous hitter, you would be wise to take a pitch to force him to throw a strike. Also, a pitcher who has difficulty throwing a breaking ball for a strike is a guy you can be very selective with. Even if he gets ahead of you, he may be forced to stay with the fastball because of his inability to throw the breaking ball. If you are the hitter with a good basestealer on first, it is a good idea to take early in the count so that the runner has a chance to steal the base. If the runner does not steal, your chances of seeing fastballs remains fairly good because the catcher wants a chance to throw the runner out and his best chance comes on something hard.

Managers should not be afraid to put the take sign

on. The score and inning situations that exist should dictate to the manager when the take sign is in order. For example, if your team is trailing by two runs late in the game, you should have your hitters take until they get a strike on them when the bases are empty. If a runner gets on, then the tying run comes to the plate and you would probably let the hitter swing away, especially if he has long-ball potential. The whole idea behind taking pitches is to try to create runners on base in order to have the potential for a big inning. That is why hitters should take more pitches when their team is trailing. Make the pitcher work to get through each inning. Make him throw a lot of pitches, especially late in the game, to get you out.

CHAPTER 7

TEACHING TECHNIQUE

Perhaps the most difficult thing for amateur coaches and managers to do with young players is to teach them the proper way to do things on the baseball field. What I will try to accomplish in this chapter is to touch on some areas that I have not already discussed in other chapters of this manual.

1. GRIPPING THE BASEBALL - Players of all levels have difficulties throwing the ball so that it does not sail or "run" on them, especially longer throws. Many times, this is a result of an improper grip on the ball. The ball is designed with the seams running in an ovular pattern around the ball. Depending how these seams are gripped, the ball will travel through the air in different ways. The ideal grip releases the ball in such a way as to cause the ball to come out of the fingers with back spin, so that the horseshoe shapes formed by the seams are rotating backwards. To accomplish this the thrower must grip the ball across the seams. The forefinger and middle finger should be placed over the far seam of the horseshoe and the thumb should be placed directly under the ball so that the inside edge of the thumb is in contact with the ball. The near edge seam of the horseshoe will touch the two fingers around the base of the fingers. When the ball is released from this grip, the result should be a backspinning ball coming off the finger tips.

2. THE THROWING MOTION - To help the player throw the ball so that it does not tail, a release point as far over the top needs to be strived for. This, in addition to the proper grip, will result in a strong, accurate throw. To get over the top, a player needs to think of getting his elbow up to the same level as his ear. By doing this, the player has forced himself to release the ball higher and thus will have more carry on his throw.

Throwing techniques are different, depending on the position the player plays. By this I mean that there are certain positions that demand a "short-arm" technique and others that require a "long-arm" technique. Generally speaking, the longer throws need to be long armed and the shorter, quicker throws need to be short armed. Pitchers and outfielders should be long armers and infielders and catchers short armers. The difference between the two is quite simple. The long arm technique has the player forming a large arc by taking the ball from his glove and extending his arm back behind him

149

before coming over the top to throw. The short arm technique has the player taking the ball from the glove directly up to the elbow at ear position. This obviously is the quicker of the two techniques and is needed most of the time on the infield for the shorter, quick throws.

3. CATCHING THE BALL - You often hear scouts refer to players as having "good" or "bad" hands. This is in reference to how they catch the ball. To get to the highest levels of the game a player needs to develop soft hands, and proper technique can help him attain this. As a thrown ball or batted ball approaches the fielder, the fielder should attempt to catch the ball out in front of his body and "give" or absorb the impact of the ball by bringing the ball back towards his body as the catch is made. This also helps to create a rhythm for the ensuing throw that may have to be made. If the ball is above the waist, the fingers of the glove should be pointed skyward. When the ball is coming below the waist the fingers should be pointing down. On a pop-up or fly ball, always try to position yourself behind where you think the ball would land so that you can have some momentum moving forward as the catch is made. It is always a good practice to have both hands up for the catch so that you can quickly get the ball out of the glove after the catch.

4. FIELDING A GROUND BALL - The biggest obstacle that players of all levels have to overcome when fielding grounders is the fear factor. This can only be done by taking hundreds of ground balls. If a player is willing to do this, then his chances of becoming adept on ground balls greatly increases. A few tips concerning technique should help. First, it is very important to be in a comfortable, ready position as the pitch is approaching the hitter. This should always be a position that has the knees slightly bent and the hands out in front of the body. Your feet should be about shoulder width apart and you should be moving in towards the hitter as the pitch is made. Once the ground ball is hit at you, continue to "creep" in until you determine where the short hop of the ground ball will take place. When you have determined this, you may have to speed up or slow down so that you can get your glove to the spot of the short hop. You should always try to field the ball just as it hits the ground and begins to come up, that is the short hop. Keep the feet shoulder width apart and bend the knees more to lower yourself into fielding position; don't bend your back forward but rather keep your back as straight as possible while bending your knees. At the moment you field the ball, your glove should be in a position that has the fingers at or near the ground with the palm of the glove slightly in front and over the top of your fingers. Your feet and glove should form a triangle. Try to field the ball as far out in front of you as possible so that you can see both the oncoming ball and your glove. As you field the ball, again bring the ball back to your body to create rhythm for the throw. If the ground ball is off to the side, you may not be able to get in front of it. In this case, your footwork to prepare for the throw is important. Always try to get to your pivot foot (right foot for right-handed throwers) before making the throw.

5. CROW HOP - This is a term used to describe the momentum creating technique that fielders use to execute a throw. If the fielder is moving in as he fields the ball, as he should be, the crow hop is merely an extension of this momentum. For an infielder, the crow hop serves two important purposes. First, it gets him moving in the direction of his throw which helps his accuracy. Second, it creates momentum for him which helps the velocity of his throw. Once the infielder has cradled the ball back to his body as discussed earlier, his next move is to continue the movement by making a small hop onto his pivot foot in the direction of his target. As he lands on his pivot foot, his arm should be in position to execute the throw. Some fielders take more than one crow hop to create more forward momentum and a stronger throw. This is okay as long as they have the time to do this.

Outfielders also must use a form of the crow hop to help them get more on their throws. When charging a ground ball, the outfielder should attempt to field the ball with his non-pivot foot out front so that he can field the ball and hop onto his pivot foot and throw. This will take some repetition to perfect, but the results will be no wasted steps before the throw.

Turning a double play, pages 154 to 157. Shortstop coming across bag. Notice hands out front to receive throw. Right foot drags across corner of bag.

Second baseman set up for double play. Notice hands out front, knees bent, left foot on bag.

Step to throw with right foot, hands out front.

Pivot on right foot, step to first with left foot. Notice
distance from the bag. Short arm throw.

Across the "horseshoe" grip. Prevents the ball from sailing.
Notice finger tips on seams, thumb under ball.

Short-arm throw. Notice elbow up and ball to ear area.

Long-arm throw. Notice elbow back and ball pointed away from target.

Receiving throw on the tag play. Notice straddle of the
bag, hands out front.

Fielding ground ball. Notice knees bent to lower fielder.
Triangle formed by feet and glove. Field ball out front.
Glove hand tilted palm over fingers. Use two hands.

Catching pop-up or fly ball. Notice set-up is behind where ball will land. Catch ball out front. Use two hands.

CLOSING COMMENTS

I truly hope that this manual has proved to be helpful to you, its readers. My recommendation is to use it as a tool to better prepare yourself as a player or instructor, or even to just better educate yourself as a fan of the game. When the game is played the right way, it is really a thing of beauty to watch. Thank you for reading this manual and good luck in your baseball future!